C000285753

Archaeology Walks in The Peak District

Ali Cooper

Copyright © A. Cooper, 1999, reprinted 2004;
reprinted with revisions 2006

All Rights Reserved. No part of this publication may be reproduced, stored in a retrieval system, or transmitted in any form or by any means – electronic, mechanical, photocopying, recording, or otherwise – without prior written permission from the publisher or a licence permitting restricted copying issued by the Copyright Licensing Agency, 90 Tottenham Court Road, London W1P 0LA. This book may not be lent, resold, hired out or otherwise disposed of by trade in any form of binding or cover other than that in which it is published, without the prior consent of the publisher.

Published by Sigma Leisure – an imprint of
Sigma Press, 5 Alton Road, Wilmslow, Cheshire SK9 5DY, England.

British Library Cataloguing in Publication Data
A CIP record for this book is available from the British Library.

ISBN: 1-85058-707-8

Typesetting and Design by: Sigma Press, Wilmslow, Cheshire.

Cover photographs: *main picture* – a crouched burial being excavated; *smaller pictures, from top* – the chambered tomb at Green Low, Aldwark; 'Freaks in the Peaks' Morris dancing at Arbor Low; excavations on Gardom's Edge in June 1998 *(Ali Cooper)*.

Maps and photographs: Ali Cooper

Printed by: Progress Press, Malta

Disclaimer: the information in this book is given in good faith and is believed to be correct at the time of publication. No responsibility is accepted by either the author or publisher for errors or omissions, or for any loss or injury howsoever caused. Only you can judge your own fitness, competence and experience.

Preface

This book of walks is written for people with an interest in archaeology. The routes are focused around ancient features, built by man, that are still visible in the landscape. Most of the archaeological sites visited are prehistoric – that is to say they were built before we had written records of the past, from Britain's point of view this means before the Roman invasion. A few, such as castles and medieval manors and granges, are more recent.

In my descriptions, I have tried to be factual – as far as that is possible in archaeology. As such, I have included details of excavations and the artefacts discovered, sometimes citing comparisons with finds and features in other parts of the country. The book is not about my opinions or theories, it is for the reader and walker to look at the evidence and make up their own mind about how we lived in the past.

The walks vary greatly in their content. Some areas, such as Stanton Moor and Gardom's Edge, are very rich in archaeological remains and as such have attracted close scrutiny by archaeologists; in other areas, features of interest may be some miles apart. Many of the walks are quite long with optional shorter routes. To avoid repeating text, the bulk of the archaeological description is included in the main walks, shorter strolls are listed immediately after (labelled a, or b) and most have their own map and instructions but direct the reader to join the main walk at appropriate points.

Route descriptions are often brief (finding the way is, after all, half the fun!) and obviously a sketch map cannot show every wall and stile. It is therefore essential to carry the relevant Ordnance Survey map and preferably a compass.

Ali Cooper

Acknowledgements

Many thanks are due to . . .

Everyone who taught me about archaeology, especially to Con and to Hamish,

Karen, who taught me about writing.

My fellow walkers – Bryan; Chris and Dan; Don, Carol and Katy; Nick; Steve and Yvonne,

B & A Photographic in Eastwood.

I would also like to acknowledge the work done by Trent and Peak Archaeological Trust, the Peak Park Authority, Sheffield University Department of Archaeology and all the other archaeologists, past and present, whose efforts have contributed so much to our understanding of the history and prehistory of the Peak District.

Changes in the Peak District – 2006 updates

In the seven years since this book was first published there have been some changes in the Peak District. The visitor centre at Edale is currently being redeveloped to incorporate a field study centre. It is due to reopen summer 2006. Meanwhile, a new visitor centre has opened just down the road at Castleton. On Stanton Moor there has been a recent survey/excavation of the Nine Ladies stone circle (p72) and at Dove Holes the Bull Ring henge has been the subject of a geophysical survey (p144).

The most up-to-date book on the area is *The Peak District: Landscapes through time* by John Barnatt and Ken Smith. This is a revised edition of their 1997 English Heritage book. In addition, much information is now available on the internet, eg the PDNPA website at www.peakdistrict-nationalpark.info/.

Contents

Archaeological Background   1

    Late Upper Palaeolithic: 12000-8000BC   1

    Mesolithic: 8000-4000BC   2

    Neolithic: 4000-2000BC   2

    Bronze Age: 2000-700BC   3

    Iron Age: 700BC-AD50   4

    Romans and Romano-British: AD43-450   4

    Anglo-Saxons and Danes: AD400-900   5

    Mid and Later Medieval: AD1000+   5

    Finding out more about Archaeology   6

    Safety, Conservation and the Countryside Code   6

        Walking in the Peak District   6

        Footwear   6

        Maps and Compasses   6

        Other Essentials   7

        Dogs   7

        Timing your walks   7

        Conservation and Consideration   7

        Access and Rights of Way   7

        Archaeological Features   8

The Walks

Walk 1: The Manifold Valley and Ecton Hill   9
    Distance: 8 miles (13km).

Walk 1a: The Manifold Valley Caves   16
    Distance: 4 miles (6km).

Walk 2: Long Low and Reynard's Cave   17
    Distance: 9 miles (15km)

Walk 3: Fox Hole Cave and Pilsbury Castle   23
    Distance: 7 miles (11km)

Walk 3a: Pilsbury Castle   28
    Distance: 4 miles (7km)

Walk 4: Barrows near the Tissington Trail   29
Distance: 3½ miles (5.5km)

Walk 5: Wigber Low and Bradbourne   34
Distance: 4½ miles (7km)

Walk 6: Rainster Rocks and Harborough Rocks   38
Distance: 5½ miles (9km)

Walk 7. Minning Low and Roystone Grange   43
Distance: 5 miles (8km)

Walk 8: Green Low   50
Distance: 4 miles (6km)

Walk 9: Arbor Low and Ringham Low   54
Distance: 9 miles (14km)

Walk 10: Stanton Moor and Harthill Moor   61
Distance: 8½ miles (13.5km)

Walk 10a: Stanton Moor and Doll Tor Stone Circle   70
Distance: 3½ miles (5.5km)

Walk 10b: Harthill Moor   73
Distance: 3½ miles (5.5km)

Walk 11: Crane's Fort and Conksbury   74
Distance: 7 miles (11km)

Walk 12: Fin Cop   79
Distance: 7½ miles (12km)

Walk 13: Five Wells, Deepdale and Chee Tor   84
Distance: 11 miles (17.5km)

Walk 13a: Five Wells and Thirst Hole Cave   93
Distance: 8 miles (13km) or 4 miles (6km)

Walk 13b: Chee Tor and Miller's Dale   95
Distance: 3½ miles (5.5km)

Walk 14: Beeley Moor   97
Distance: 6 miles (10km)

Walk 15: Gardom's Edge   103
        Distance: 3 miles (5km)

Walk 16: The Edges – Baslow, Curbar and Froggatt   108
        Distance: 11 miles (18km)

Walk 17: Cairns and Circles on Eyam Moor   114
        Distance: 10 miles (16km) or 7 miles (11km)

Walk 18: Carl Wark, Upper Padley and Hathersage   120
        Distance: 8 miles (13km)

Walk 19: Mam Tor and Navio   127
        Distance: 11 miles (18km)

Walk 19a: Mam Tor and Castleton   136
        Distance: 5 miles (8km)

Walk 19b: Castleton and Navio   139
        Distance: 5 miles (8km)

Walk 20: Castle Naze and The Bull Ring Henge   140
        Distance: 8 miles (13km)

Walk 21: Torside Castle and Doctor's Gate   146
        Distance: 14 miles (22km)

Useful Addresses and Phone Numbers   153

Glossary   154

Index   157

Location Map

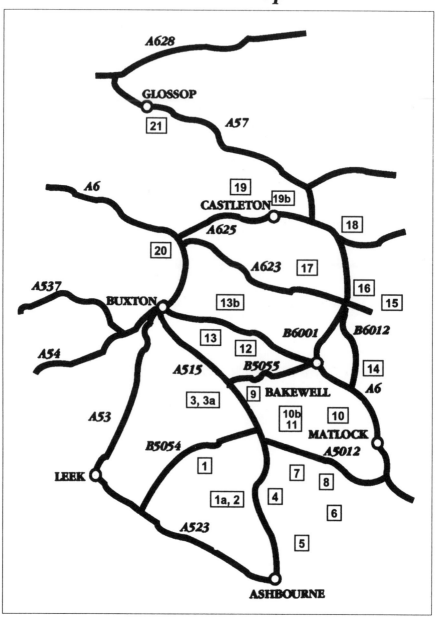

Archaeological Background

Early hominids inhabited Britain sporadically more than 500,000 years ago. However, populations were very small and almost all traces of their lives have been erased by subsequent glaciations. It is the story of the last 12,000 years, since the ice finally retreated, which we now see imprinted on the landscape around us. Like other parts of the country, the archaeology of the Peak District has always had its own regional variants. Part of this is due to geographical position, the centre of the country will receive goods imported from Europe considerably later than coastal areas; part is due to the ecology, the limestone plateau and moorlands have always been suited to a pastoral way of life. The following paragraphs offer a brief description of life in different periods of history and prehistory, with a summary of the remains they have left in the landscape today. Dates are approximate and the names given to prehistoric time zones should be regarded as a useful reference rather than descriptive of the way of life.

Late Upper Palaeolithic: 12000-8000BC

In the open, there is little to be seen of the late Upper Palaeolithic, the last period of the Old Stone Age. We know from pollen samples that vegetation began to grow back in the form of tundra, with grassland and dwarf birch; fauna at this time included horses, foxes, badgers and beaver. Animals such as lion and elephant, which shared the land with early man in previous warm periods, never returned. Although this was the beginning of the Holocene, with great changes happening across the world, we still classify human development as being part of the Palaeolithic because of the similarity of tools, mostly of stone, with those produced before. Remains from this time are mostly found in caves such as those in the Manifold Valley where a more constant environment and minimal disturbance have aided their preservation.

Mesolithic: 8000-4000BC

During the early part of the Mesolithic the land was forested with birch and pine. There were also considerable inland lakes and watercourses. Scatters of microliths, small flakes of worked flint thought to have been part of larger composite tools, indicate that man formed camps in the area and hunted animals – especially red and roe deer. Until recently it was thought that such hunter gatherer groups simply followed the herds off which they fed and did not manage the land in any way. However, more recent studies suggest that the fires (which we know occurred) were not accidental but deliberate acts to clear the woodland and so encourage grazing and growth of crops. It has been suggested that the Mesolithic people were semi-nomadic, inhabiting the uplands of the Pennines during the summer and moving east to the wolds and the seashore during the winter.

The sea level, which had been rising since the ice melted, finally covered the land bridge between Britain and Europe about 8000 years ago. Britain was now an island. The temperature was also rising and vegetation began to change from pine and birch to a mixed deciduous forest. Although this appears lusher, it is not so good for grazing and supports less wild animals. This would have put pressure on the hunters to manipulate the environment or change their lifestyle. Again, evidence of Mesolithic occupation can be seen in the Manifold Valley. Land management during this time may well have subtly influenced the landscape today and may be in part responsible for the lack of arboreal growth and subsequent development of peat bogs on the higher uplands.

Neolithic: 4000-2000BC

The most noticeable landscape sites of earthworks and standing stones date from the Neolithic and Bronze Age. The limestone of the area of White Peak was covered with fine fertile soil. This, combined with a prolific supply of freshwater springs would have made it very appealing to the early farmers, both for growing cereals and for grazing sheep (recently introduced from Europe), cattle and pigs.

At the beginning of this period, the area (including the now barren hillsides) was dominated by oak woodland. Hazel grew as a low shrub and was coppiced to make hurdles, while elm was probably used for animal fodder. Lower land, near water, supported alder and willow. Neolithic people cleared much of the land by methods such as ring-barking (cutting a deep incision around the circumference of a tree trunk, eventually causing the plant to die).

The old English word 'low' is rather misleading in that it refers to a high point, usually round or conical in shape. It can indicate either a burial mound or a hill and is more often than not a combination of both. During the Neolithic, the structure beneath the barrow often took the form of a chambered tomb, a stone construction in which an entrance passage led to ante-rooms containing different bones. This was not so much a final resting place for individuals as a repository for a selection of remains, denoting territory and making bones available for use in ceremonies. After many decades of such 'use', these tombs were eventually closed. Neolithic and Bronze Age burial mounds are often found in close proximity and sometimes built in alignment.

Dating from the later Neolithic (about 2000 – 2500BC), henges are circular earthworks of banks and ditches with one or more gaps in the bank. Occasionally, as at Arbor Low, a stone circle is built inside the henge at a later date. In the Peak District, henges and stone circles tend to have a later date than similar monuments in other parts of the country. Some archaeologists ascribe them to a particular period based on the date while others will say that, for example, a henge is late Neolithic because it reflects the behaviour typical of that time. Another way of describing this would be to say that the late Neolithic, Early Bronze Age etc came late to the Peak District.

Bronze Age: 2000-700BC

Most stone circles and round burial mounds date to the Early Bronze Age. The axes of such monuments often have astronomical alignments. The early Bronze Age is known for the emergence of the Beaker culture. We cannot be sure whether this took the form of an invasion of people or the adoption of new ideas but we can be certain that the hallmarks of this culture – finely decorated pottery, bronze working and the recognition of individuals for their particular trades and skills – originated in Europe.

The use of bronze is significant because of the technology required to produce it. Artefacts found include items of jewellery and weapons such as daggers and axes. The alloys produced were quite soft and it is likely that objects of metal were seen as prestige goods rather than being useful in an everyday sense. The main material used for tools was still stone.

The Later Bronze Age saw a marked deterioration in the climate with colder, wetter weather. This may have some bearing on the appearance of fortified settlements such as Mam Tor. This and similar encampments were used into the Iron Age with their defences reinforced.

Iron Age: 700BC-AD50

The use of iron for tools was a great technological advance. The farmsteads or smallholdings suggest a way of life we can to some extent identify with. The Iron Age signifies an increase in population combined with a downturn in the weather, it is also clear that clans or chiefdoms were forming, creating a structured and to some extent class-based society. It is hardly surprising then that defence of land and property became more important, hence the building of fortified hilltop enclosures. There are several hillforts to see in the Peak District and one or two settlements probably spanning the Iron Age and Roman period have been identified. However, apart from hillforts, the type of structures built at this time do not stand out so obviously in the landscape as those of the preceding millennia. They are more likely to be seen as crop marks in cultivated fields.

The uplands seem to have been abandoned for cultivation around this time, presumably trees were not regenerating and the process of peat formation was under way. The emphasis is still very much on a pastoral economy and the archaeological record of the Iron Age in this area lacks the huge hillforts or rich chariot burials found in other parts of the country.

Romans and Romano-British: AD50-350

In the main it was the culture of these people and not the individuals themselves who hailed from Rome. Archaeologists tend to ascribe the label of Roman to the army, forts, roads etc and to artefacts such as coins. The Romano-British were the descendants of Iron Age people rather than immigrants; they continued to live under Roman occupation. In some parts of the country, the native Britons became very Romanised with the richest landowners and chiefs occupying villas.

In the Peak District, with the exception of lead mining, it is likely that the pastoral way of life continued much as before. A local form of Romano-British pottery known as Derbyshire Ware was produced and this was in general use. The Romans were interested in generating income and, in most parts of the country, the main source probably was arable farming. In the Peak District, however, their interest was in the large supply of lead ore, and after the initial invasion it is likely that forts in this region were concerned with policing this enterprise. Several settlement sites in the Peak date to Iron Age or Romano-British occupation.

Anglo-Saxons and Danes: AD400-900

In the period historically known as the Dark Ages there were successive waves of immigrants and goods from Europe. Christianity reached Britain in the seventh century but each group of newcomers was initially pagan, converting to Christianity after a short time. This can be seen in their burials – e.g. some Anglo-Saxons were buried in barrows; the practice of including grave goods, especially items such as swords indicates pagan beliefs. The Peak District Anglo-Saxons or Peak-Dwellers as they are sometimes known are regarded as having their own local culture. Many stone-carved crosses date to this time and most were probably wayside shrines, being relocated to churchyards later. Many place names derive from Anglo-Saxon or Danish times as do the layouts of towns and villages.

Mid and Later Medieval: AD1000+

Although this book is mostly concerned with prehistory, a few more recent sites are visited. From Norman times onwards there is considerable evidence of rich manorial centres. The beginnings of these are seen as ringworks, and later as motte and bailey constructions, but the architecture was soon based in stone with longer-lasting buildings such as Peveril Castle. The other wealthy landowners in the

the area were monasteries. They continued the pastoral theme with granges, farms managed by lay-brethren. The absentee landowners were usually abbeys based in surrounding counties so, as in Roman times, the income was going elsewhere.

Finding out more about Archaeology

The most definitive book on the archaeology of the Peak is *The Peak District: Landscapes through time* by John Barnatt and Ken Smith (Windgather Press 2004) . In addition, each walk in this book is followed by a short list of suggested reading for those wishing to read in more detail about the places they have visited. Many of these are reports printed in archaeological journals, notably the Derbyshire Archaeological Journal (DAJ), its predecessor the Derbyshire Archaeological and Natural History Society Journal (DANHSJ) and the North Staffordshire Journal of Field Studies (NSJFS). These are available in public libraries in the relevant counties and in University libraries throughout the country. The references are a selection of the literature available rather than a complete bibliography of research material. You may also wish to see some of the artefacts mentioned and many of these are on display in local museums, especially Sheffield and Buxton.

Safety, Conservation and the Countryside Code

Walking in the Peak District

Most of the walks in this book are in rural areas with small farms and villages, you will usually not be far from civilisation. If you are planning a longer route on the moors then be sure to check the weather forecast and, particularly if you are walking alone, tell someone where you are going and what time you expect to return.

Footwear

During the winter, walking boots are always advisable although wellington boots would suffice for shorter walks. In the summer, providing it is dry, trainers or strong flat shoes with good treads may be adequate.

Maps and Compasses

The sketch maps and directions in this book are indicators of particular routes but they are not a substitute for a full map. For walks 1-17 you should carry the Ordnance Survey Outdoor Leisure 24 (1:25000) and for walks 19 and 21 Outdoor Leisure 1 (1:25000). Walks 18 and 20 require both maps. A compass is always useful to clarify your position and is essential for walks on open moorland. During my research for this book I have frequently been asked directions from walkers following guide books, not only because they are unsure of their route but sometimes because they want to take a short cut back to their cars.

Other Essentials

Always take a small backpack containing food, drink, a waterproof and an extra layer of clothing such as a jumper or sweatshirt. In the winter, make sure you carry a flask of hot drink or soup. For evening or winter walks you may also wish to carry a small torch in case you do not return to your car until after dusk.

Dogs

There are sheep or cows grazing in most fields and sheep on the open moorland. Some of the areas you will visit contain deep mine shafts and precipitous cliffs. You should therefore keep dogs on a lead at all times.

Timing your walks

Everyone walks at their own pace so distances rather than duration have been given for each route. If you walk at a moderate pace you will probably need to allow at least half an hour per mile to give time to explore the features along the way. Extra time should be allowed for breaks, especially on longer routes.

Conservation and Consideration

Most field boundaries are crossed via stiles but please make sure you close gates securely where appropriate. If you stop to picnic, take all litter home with you.

Access and Rights of Way

As far as possible these walks are planned around public rights of way, such routes are protected by law and should always be open. Sometimes the way is via concessionary paths or across open access land. In these cases, either a route has been negotiated with the land-owner or the land is owned by the Peak National Park and access cannot always be guaranteed. Some areas of moorland have been deemed ecologically or archaeologically fragile and are closed to the public to protect them from accidental or intentional damage. At present, this restriction applies to Big Moor and a large section of Beeley Moor which is why there are no walks in this book visiting Swine Sty or the Barbrook stone circles. Anyone with a particular interest in these areas should apply in writing to the Peak Park Authority in Bakewell for permission to visit.

In many cases, sites on private land can be viewed from a nearby road or footpath. Sometimes, though, it is necessary to cross a short distance of private land to explore a feature satisfactorily. In this situation, it is up to the individual reader and walker to seek permission from the landowner as they see fit and to take responsibility for their own actions.

Archaeological Features

Too many Peak District archaeological sites have been accidentally or intentionally damaged. Please take great care when you are exploring. Do not deface or climb over stones and barrows or remove artefacts. Please respect the places you visit so that they will remain for future generations to see.

Walk 1: The Manifolð Valley anð Ecton Hill

Distance: 8 miles (13km).

Starting Point: Hulme End, SK103593. Park next to the visitor centre at Hulme End, this is the start of the Manifold Way.

Refreshments: There is a tea shop at Wetton Mill and pubs in Wetton and Hulme End.

Alternative Routes: Walk 1a, a shorter route of 4 miles, starts in Wetton and visits the Manifold Valley.

Preamble

The Manifold Valley caves have produced artefacts from as long ago as the Late Upper Palaeolithic – the end of the last ice age – and faunal remains from even further back. Ecton Hill has archaeology from the Bronze Age as well as copper mines, at least one of which has recently been restored. Almost half of the walk is on the level path of the Manifold Way but there are also some very steep hills to climb. Walkers are strongly advised not to attempt to explore inside the cave entrances apart from Thor's – anyone wishing to look further underground should join a reputable cave or mine exploration club (see useful addresses). This walk is planned so that you can benefit from the facilities of the visitor centre at the start, stop for lunch at the Royal Oak at Wetton and for afternoon tea at Wetton Mill. Long distance visitors can then spend the evening at the Manifold Inn at Hulme End, having first pitched their tents in the campsite opposite.

The Walk

From the visitor centre, turn right onto the road and walk the few hundred metres to the bridge, cross the river and turn right into the lane signposted to Wetton. After a few minutes, take the turning to the right then follow the footpath to the left immediately after the

The caves on the clifftop have a commanding view of the Manifold Valley

first house, crossing a stile in the middle of the field boundary opposite. Carry on in this direction (south-south-west) until you come
out onto the road. Turn left onto the road then go up the farm track
(as indicated by a post) immediately after the farm building on the
right. Cross the next two fields diagonally and you should come out
at a bend in the road, turn sharp right onto a track leading up the hill
– you have almost doubled back on yourself. You will soon come to
an old stone hut in a rather exposed north-facing position.

You are now on Ecton Hill, the Peak District's source of copper
ore. The mine workings here also produced lead in the form of galena in the higher levels. For the next section of the walk I have suggested a route down the east side of the hill. However, other rights of
way are marked and those interested in industrial archaeology may
wish to explore the hilltop more thoroughly before proceeding to
Wetton Hill. On the west side you can see the remains of Ecton and
Swainsley mines.

Cross a stile and turn immediately left, following the wall up the
hill, if you veer slightly to the right (approximately due south) you

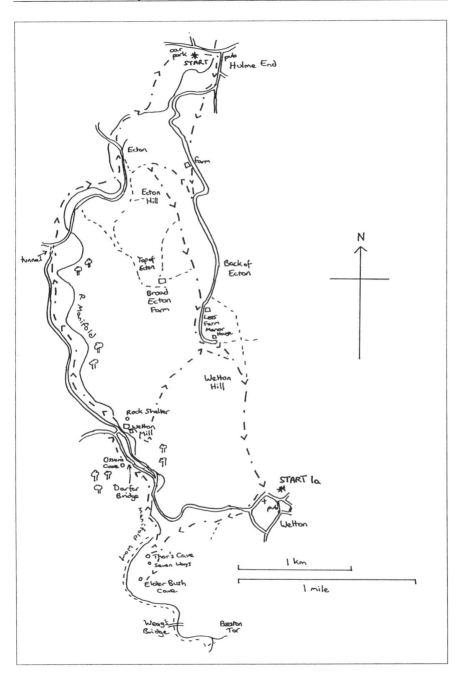

will come to the trig point on the summit. The area is sprinkled with old mine shafts. The copper ore here was generally found in the deeper levels, if you drop a stone down you will appreciate the need for the fences and grids! Without closer inspection, the upcast from the workings can easily be mistaken for barrows. Mine workings are notoriously difficult to date. Occasionally archaeologists are lucky enough to find an abandoned face with digging implements nearby, sometimes it is possible to tell from the face what type of tools were used on it. Usually, however, all evidence is destroyed by more recent mineral extraction. We know that Ecton Hill was occupied as far back as the Bronze Age from the presence of barrows and stone tools; as yet, we have know way of knowing whether the copper ore was exploited at that time.

Continue down the path, you will soon cross a stile near to considerable mine workings and ruined buildings. Waterbank mine immediately on your left was one of the major enterprises of the seventy or so mine workings on the hill. The way begins to descend now and the path joins a farm track. Turn left, down the hill and right onto the roadway. In front you can see Wetton Hill and the way ahead is between the two peaks. The lane bends to the left, passing Lees Farm and the Manor House, then a footbridge – or rather substantial stepping stones – give access to the National Trust land around Wetton Hill.

➡ *Walkers on the short route from Wetton rejoin here*

The path leads south-east, hugging the wall on the right, then turns with the boundary to take a more southerly direction. At the end of the next section of wall there are two stiles, one leading diagonally across the field ahead, the other turning right to the summit of Wetton Hill.

At this point, fans of hill walking may like to take a short detour to the top of Wetton Hill, to the site of the barrow there. Although there is not much left to see of the archaeology, there are magnificent views and it gives an insight into the minds of the people who chose to bury their dead in such a commanding place. Standing on the summit, it makes sense to regard the barrows of prehistoric burials as much more than graves but rather a declaration of territory and power. If you look due east, you may also be able to make out the three barrows on the distant hillside.

Return to the path that leads the half-mile into Wetton. If you want to stop at the Royal Oak, then you should go straight ahead when you join the road, otherwise turn right and follow the signs to Wetton Mill and Thor's Cave.

➡*Walkers on the short trip to the Manifold Caves start here*

As you bear right on the road out of Wetton you can see Thor's Cave in the cliff-face ahead. The way to the entrance is signposted up a track to the left. A short distance up this narrow lane, a sign directs you over a stile to the right. The path turns left, following the wall you have just crossed, then twists across the field, climbing up towards the huge archway.

At this point, make sure that children and dogs are secured on leads. The cliffs ahead can be very dangerous with unexpected precipitous drops.

Just before the cave the path divides with the right-hand fork leading to the cave entrance and the steps down to the valley and the left-hand route leading to the clifftop above. I strongly recommend a detour to the top here but do take care – the most obvious path leads steeply uphill then ends abruptly at a sheer drop! From this topmost point, you can see Seven Ways Cave with its multiple entrances. You can approach it by circling round to the left. The interior is now collapsed but the small cavern was once used for a Neolithic burial (although only a few bones were found) and several thousand years later for a Saxon interment.

In the steep hillside between Thor's and Seven Ways (don't attempt to find the entrance!) Thor's Fissure Cave was found to be very rich archaeologically. Flint tools from the Late Upper Palaeolithic – the end of the last ice age – were found, together with the bones of reindeer and red deer. Other finds in the cave, dating to the Beaker period (about 2000BC) included a polished stone axe and, rather surprisingly, dolphin bones. There were also artefacts from Iron Age and Roman times.

Further along the clifftop is Elder Bush Cave, popular with cavers because of its fine decorations (if you want to look inside do so with a reputable caving club). This shelter contained a cache of reindeer bones covered by rocks. Archaeologists interpret it as a store of meat placed there between ten and twelve thousand years ago. Again, artefacts from more recent times were found.

Return to Thor's Cave. This is safe to explore if you are careful but beware of the 'window' with the steep drop outside. The cave contained a crouched burial in a cist from the Later Neolithic (2500-2000BC) and evidence of Romano-British occupation. This was certainly a dwelling with a view.

From the ledge outside the cave, take the steps and then the path down to the valley. A footbridge crosses the almost always dry river-bed – the water has gone underground further upstream. A well-maintained path leads to another bridge. Cross to the west side of the River Manifold and turn right, following the path to the north. Where the lane branches into two parallel roadways, take the one on the left.

About a mile from the footbridge you come to Darfar Bridge. Pause on the bridge and look to the hillside on your left. At the top of a grassy slope, at the base of the cliff is Ossum's Cave. Reindeer bones dating to the Late Upper Palaeolithic (10000-12000 years ago) were found here. At first it was thought they represented human occupation but after subsequent re-examination the site is now interpreted as a wolf kill. The reindeer do, however, give an indication of the cold climate and some archaeologists believe they were on a seasonal migration from the Welsh borders to Germany – Britain was joined to Europe by a landbridge – and that the people may have visited the area occasionally, perhaps following the herds.

Carry on along the road, crossing the ford, then turn right to Wetton Mill. This is a good place to stop for a snack or a cup of tea. The shop also sells guides to the Manifold Valley caves.

Before you go, take the path up behind the mill buildings and turn left to Wetton Mill rock shelter. On excavation, this had evidence of human occupation in Mesolithic times (8000 years ago). Lower levels of the floor contained bones of glutton (wolverine), arctic fox and lemmings indicating a glacial period.

➨***Walkers on route 1a should return to those instructions now***

Return to level ground and go back across the bridge to the Manifold Way. The river, which has much more water and indeed sometimes floods at this point, is so named because it has many folds, that is, it meanders a lot. The next mile and a half is, unfortunately, joined by a road so watch out for traffic. Continue through the tunnel. Ecton Bridge is on your right and more disused mines can be seen on the west side of Ecton Hill from now on.

When the road crosses to the other side of the river, continue straight ahead on the footpath. It is now an easy level walk back to the car park.

Finding out more:

Bramwell, D 1973 *Archaeology in the Peak District: a guide to the region's prehistory* (Moorland Publishing, Buxton)

Bramwell, D 1964 'The Excavations at Elder Bush Cave, Wetton, Staffs' *North Staffordshire Journal of Field Studies*. Vol 4.

Robey J A & L Porter 1972 *The Copper and Lead Mines of Ecton Hill, Staffordshire* (Moorland Publishing and Peak District Mine Historic Society)

Walk 1a: The Manifold Valley Caves

Distance: 4 miles (6km).

Starting Point: Wetton, SK109553. Park in the village of Wetton. This is best approached from Alstonefield or Hulme End.

Refreshments: There is a tea shop at Wetton Mill and a pub in Wetton.

Preamble

This short stroll enables you to see some of the Manifold Valley caves, returning via Wetton Hill.

The Walk

➡*Join instructions for walk 1 where indicated.*

After visiting Wetton Mill rock shelter, walk due south up the hill behind the mill buildings. Turn left onto the National Trust land of Wetton Hill following the stream between the higher peaks, Wetton Hill is on your right and Sugarloaf on your left. Just before the buildings on the left, cross the stream and bear right to join the path that runs down the east side of Wetton Hill.

➡*Rejoin walk 1 where indicated.*

Walk 2: Long Low and Reynard's Cave

Distance: 9 miles (15km)

Starting Point: Alstonefield SK131556 or Milldale SK139547. Park in the village of Alstonefield or in Milldale.

Refreshments: There is a refreshment kiosk in Milldale and pubs in Alstonefield and Hope. There is also a tea room at Ilam Hall (when open) and a kiosk in the Ilam car park.

Alternative routes: This walk is described both from Alstonefield and Milldale as it is a very popular area and there is limited parking. The route from Milldale is marginally shorter.

Preamble

This walk begins with a pleasant stroll beside the River Dove, first through Milldale and then into Dovedale to visit Reynard's Cave. The route continues along the river to Ilam then heads across to Castern and north to the huge barrow of Long Low. The walk is enjoyable at any time of year, although the hillside around Long Low is rather bleak in cold or windy weather.

The Walk

Like Castleton, Alstonefield is built around a market place and similarly it is thought to have housed an old manorial centre. Its history is clearly pre-Norman, with fragments of Anglo-Danish crosses built into the walls of the church. From Alstonefield, take the lane leading south-east from the pub. Turn right onto the footpath after the church. This route crosses several fields diagonally before descending steeply down a grassy meadow into the hamlet of Milldale where you may wish to look at the National Trust display in the building to the west of the bridge. Cross the bridge and follow the riverside path south, passing the footbridge, until you come to an area of rocky

Reynard's Cave lies beyond the rock arch

crags and caves. The path is supported by a board-walk as it passes the cliffs on the left, then opens out onto a wooded area.

High up on your left, now 120ft (36 metres) above the present river level, is the natural arch that forms the gateway to Reynard's Cave beyond. To find the cave entrance, make your way up the track and through the arch, then continue along the ledge until you come to the opening. The interior was partially excavated in 1959, producing finds as far back as the Bronze Age and possibly the Neolithic. Romano-British artefacts including a bronze fibula were also discovered and medieval people had left behind arrows and fragments of millstone and pottery. You can see some of the artefacts from Reynard's Cave on display in Buxton museum.

Carry on along the riverside path, passing the distinctive crags of Tissington Spires on your left. The route leaves the water's edge for a few hundred metres and climbs a hill. At a sharp bend to the right, a river crossing is formed by stepping stones and the main path now continues on the other side. However, unless the water level is very low you may prefer to continue along the west bank and cross by the footbridge a quarter of a mile further on.

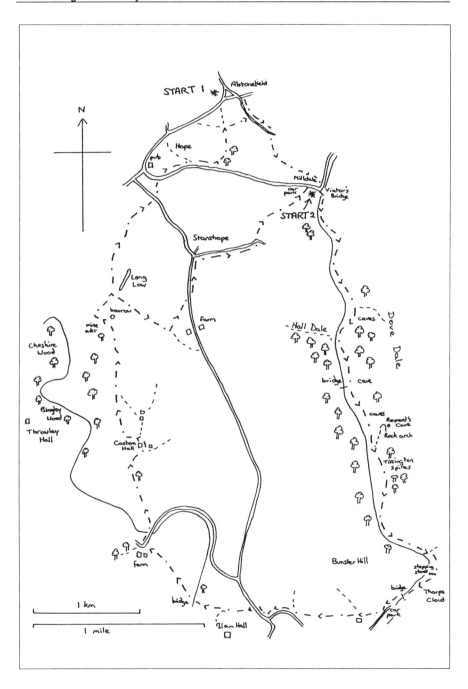

Turn left and follow the path to the car park, bearing right opposite the car park entrance to take the grassy steps that lead onto the path due west towards Ilam. Rejoin the road near Ilam Hall, leaving Bunster Hill on your right. Turn right at the junction, Home Farm should be on your right and Ilam Hall on your left. Take the footpath on the left immediately after the Hall. Follow the obvious track until it turns sharply to the left, at this point you should continue straight ahead, and in a few hundred metres cross the river via the footbridge. On the other side, bear right across the fields until you come to a road (half a mile). Turn right onto the road and cross Rushley Bridge then take the footpath on the left, this crosses several fields diagonally and, near the top of the hill, joins the track to Castern Hall. Follow the driveway, passing the main building on your left, then turn left (heading west), leaving the further cottages of Castern on your right. This path soon curves round to the right (heading north) and there are spectacular views of the hillside on the far side of the river to your left.

If you stop and look to your left you can see Throwley Hall – the remains of an earlier building are in front of the present day farm. On Mere Hill, behind the hall, is an obvious barrow. A number of burial mounds have been excavated and recorded in the Ilam and Calton area although many can no longer be located, having succumbed to damage through erosion and ploughing. However, reports suggest that most contained primary burials in the form of crouched inhumations, suggesting a Late Neolithic or Early Bronze Age date.

Continue along the path. On the near side of the river is a large disused mine adit and the forested area on the opposite bank is Cheshire Wood. High on this hillside, Cheshire Wood Cave contained the burials of at least two adults and children together with potsherds and animal bones, the upper layers contained Romano-British and possible Iron Age pottery. A quarter of a mile beyond Cheshire Wood, Falcon Low Cave contained the remains of two adults and four children thought to date from the Neolithic.

The path continues to the left of the field wall directly ahead then bears left towards the cliff edge. You should now find signposts to Wetton to the left and to Stanshope down a track to the right – take the latter. You may also notice that you are circling round a field containing an obvious barrow. After walking a few hundred metres north-east, stiles lead across a track. Long Low is opposite spanning almost two field lengths and with a stone wall running along the spine.

The extensive barrow of Long Low was originally thought to represent two round barrows connected by a ridge. Excavation now suggests that it contains a collapsed chambered tomb dating to the Later Neolithic. Within the buried stone structure were the partially articulated bones of at least thirteen individuals, animal bones and leaf-shaped arrowheads. We cannot be sure from this evidence, whether the bodies were previously lain on exposure platforms to be defleshed or whether they were buried intact. The original construction of the chambers probably looked something like those at Five Wells or Minninglow, with the huge slabs now fallen under the barrow. The entrance would probably have been at the wider end (the north-east) and it is possible there was also a horned forecourt at this end where ceremonies were performed.

If you are returning to Milldale the best route is to return across the trackway and turn south-east down the hill. Turn back and look at the silhouette of Long Low on the horizon, you get a very good appreciation of the length of the structure. After a little less than half a mile, take the path to the left which leads across to the road into Stanshope. At the junction, turn right onto the signposted track and, when this bends to the right, take the path left across the fields. An easy route now leads downhill into Milldale.

If you are returning to Alstonefield, bear left across the field (leaving Long Low on your right) and follow this left field wall north until you come to a path 'crossroads'. From here you can see the church spire in Alstonefield and the easiest method is simply to take the paths and lanes that lead in that direction! However, my preferred route is to continue ahead to the road (you should be heading north-east), take the path opposite which twists to the left across the field to join another road, then turn right. Take the second footpath on the left, opposite the track to Grove Farm. This path climbs steeply uphill then turns left. A right turn at the footpath 'crossroads' brings you out near the church.

Finding out more:

Fowler M J & J W Corcoran 1955 'The transition from Late Neolithic to Early Bronze Age in the Peak District of Derbyshire & Staffordshire' *DAJ*

Gunstone A J H 1965 'Archaeological gazetteer of Staffordshire: Part 2, the barrows' *North Staffordshire Journal of Field Studies*

Kelly J H 1960 'Excavations at Reynard's Cave, Dovedale, 1959' *DANHSJ*

Walk 3: Fox Hole Cave and Pilsbury Castle

Distance: 7 miles (11km)

Starting Point: Longnor, SK088648. Park in the village of Longnor.

Refreshments: There are refreshments available in Longnor. The Packhorse at Crowdecote offers food all day every day and accommodation.

Alternative routes: For a shorter walk, visiting Pilsbury Castle, see walk 3a.

Preamble

This walk first visits High Wheeldon, where you have the option of climbing the hill to look for Fox Hole, a cave where Neolithic people deposited pottery and the bones of a brown bear. The route continues south to explore the earthworks of Pilsbury Castle, a motte and bailey dating to Norman times. The walk continues west past Sheen Hill and returns to Longnor via the River Manifold. It is pleasant all year round but if you want to make a detour to the top of High Wheeldon then pick a summer's day with no more than a light breeze!

The Walk

You need to take the track on the eastern boundary of Longnor. To find this you can either wind your way north-east from the centre, up narrow lanes and pathways behind the craft market, or take the road out to the east and turn left onto the track immediately after the last building. After a hundred metres or so you will appreciate why this area is named Top o'th'Edge as you fork to the right down a steep slope. At the bottom of the hill the path takes a dog-leg turn to the left and right before heading north-east towards High Wheeldon, the distinctive peak a mile away. Beware! You may find the intervening low-lying ground somewhat damp underfoot.

Cross Beggar's Bridge and continue ahead. You will pass a foot-path on your right a hundred metres before the road, this will be the way on after visiting High Wheeldon. Join the lane and follow it round to the left. After a few minutes walk, a stile on the right leads onto the National Trust land of High Wheeldon Hill.

The point of interest here is Fox Hole Cave (previously known as High Wheeldon Cave) which is located near the top of the hill on the north-facing side of a limestone rib. Exploring the hillside to find the cave entrance is an optional detour, it is described as very difficult to locate and at 1250ft, the cave is one of the highest in the country. Various artefacts from different periods were found here, including Neolithic pottery and a Roman bronze armlet. There seem to have been periods of use both for occupation (two hearths were found in the entrance passage) and for burial. It is thought that the cave was treated as a long barrow in Neolithic times, with burials contained in a stone cist. This was later demolished and the space reused in Late Bronze Age and Roman times. However, there is evidence of occupa-tion before this in Late Upper Palaeolithic or Mesolithic times and animal bones dating to the late Pleistocene – the last part of the Ice Age.

Perhaps the most interesting find in the cave was the skull of a brown bear. This had been placed upside down and covered with flat slabs – a ritual practice that dates back to Mousterian times (30000-50000 years ago) and still continues in some parts of the world today. In this case, the deposition is attributed to Late Upper Palaeolithic or Mesolithic people – hunter/gatherers living between 12000-6000 years ago. Some of the finds from Fox Hole Cave can be seen in Buxton Museum.

Retrace your steps and turn left onto the path mentioned earlier. Alternatively, you can follow the road into Crowdecote where the Packhorse Inn is a good place to stop for lunch.

➡ *Walkers from Crowdecote (Walk 3a) join here*

Come out of the pub and turn left. As the road bends right towards Longnor, take the track to the left. You are directed to the right of a driveway and pass Bridge End Farm. Carry on straight ahead as the track dwindles to a path across the fields.

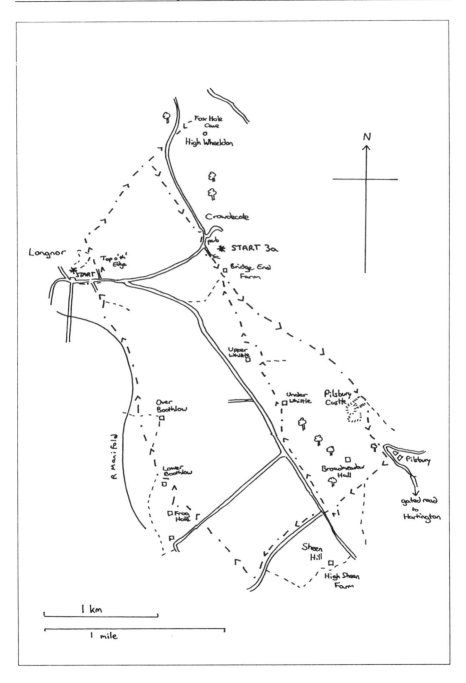

The motte and baileys of Pilsbury Castle

From here, you should be able to see Pilsbury Castle about a mile
ahead. The motte, a defensive man-made hill built to accommodate
the keep, is on the right and a natural limestone outcrop is on the
left. One of the baileys occupies the raised level area between the
two. Pilsbury Castle was built in Norman times, probably around
AD1100. In addition to the motte and baileys (you will see another
on the south side), when in use it would have had timber buildings
and palisades. The fact that it was sited at the centre of the De
Ferriers estates suggests that it may have been important adminis-
tratively, it probably went out of use after this function moved to
Hartington a century later.

There is another motte two miles to the south at Bank Top, just
beside the farm, however there is no sign of an associated bailey.
Some archaeologists interpret this as an unfinished castle, perhaps
the building was begun, then the site at Pilsbury to the north was
considered preferable, an alternative view is that both the Bank Top
earthwork and possibly the south bailey at Pilsbury were earlier
Norman features known as ringworks.

Continue along the path and cross the stile to the left of the castle; here you should turn right onto a well-established track. As you walk past the limestone knoll you can see the earthworks of a second enclosure, possibly a second bailey although this one does not enjoy the same elevated position as the first.

Much of the land in this area was under monastic ownership in medieval times. There were granges at Pilsbury, Needham and Cronkston, all owned by the Cistercian Abbey at Merevale, Warwickshire.

Continue down the track and bear right onto the lane. This is a gated road leading to Hartington. For a few metres, there is a wooded area with farm buildings on the left. When you leave the trees behind, turn right down the track and cross the ford at the bottom via a footbridge. Carry on past the footpath on the left until you climb the hill to the road.

➡ ***Walkers from Crowdecote, please return to instructions for that route (Walk 3a)***

To complete the route to Longnor, cross the road and walk down the lane opposite, passing Sheen Hill on your left. After half a mile, turn right onto the footpath, passing Hill End and emerging at another lane. Continue down the footpath opposite; this track winds to the left and right near Frog Hole and turns left, skirting to the north of the buildings at Lower Boothlow. The path now turns right and, after crossing the first field, leads down towards the River Manifold, then leaves the riverbank behind to turn up the hill into Longnor.

Finding out more:

Bramwell D 1971 'Excavations at Fox Hole Cave, High Wheeldon, 1961-1970' *DAJ*

Walk 3a: Pilsbury Castle

Distance: 4 miles (6km)

Starting Point: Crowdecote, SK101652. Park in the village of Crowdecote. There is limited roadside parking in the lane to High Wheeldon, alternatively if you go at a quiet time and buy a drink or meal at the pub the landlord will probably let you leave your car there – but please ask first!

Refreshments: The Packhorse at Crowdecote offers food all day every day and also accommodation.

Preamble

This is a gentle stroll to explore the earthworks of Pilsbury Castle, a motte and bailey dating to Norman times.

The Walk

Start at the Packhorse Inn, facing the road (not the bar!)

➡️*Join the instructions for Walk 3 where indicated.*

Turn right onto the road, there are views of Pilsbury Castle down in the valley to your right. After about one third of a mile, take the footpath on the right. This leads transversely down the slope, crossing the drive to Under Whittle farm. At the farm buildings, the path turns half left towards Upper Whittle. At the fork, bear left and continue down the hill to Bridge End Farm. Here you cross a footbridge and join the track you started on to turn left into Crowdecote.

Walk 4: Barrows near the Tissington Trail

Distance: 3½ miles (5.5km).

Starting Point: Alsop station car park, SK156548. This car park is located on the east of the A515, a mile and a half south of Newhaven. It is signposted from the road.

Refreshments: Nothing on route so make sure you take a snack! However, the Sycamore in Parwich is only a short drive away when you have completed the walk.

Preamble

The most famous barrow visited on this walk is that of Green Low, a Bronze Age Beaker burial with rich grave goods, considered to be of national importance. Several other burial sites are visited along the way and the location of Liff's Low, a Neolithic barrow with several interments each accompanied by a variety of artefacts, can be seen in the distance.

The Walk

Alsop station is on the now dismantled Tissington line. From the car park, take the footpath in the north-east corner, signposted to Alsop. Follow the path down the hill, crossing the stile into the next field but keeping to the left near the wall. You can see the village of Alsop in the valley below. The path emerges onto the road where you should turn right, continuing past the church. Take the path signposted to the left at Manor Farm. The route goes through the farmyard then over a stile. Bear left, approximately following the power lines and over a stile into the next field.

Ahead is the hill of Cross Low and the mound in the plantation to the north is labelled on Ordnance survey maps as Cross Low barrow. However, it isn't quite as simple as that! Three barrows on this

Twin peaks - clumps of trees mark two barrow sites on Cross Low, from NW

stretch of land were excavated by Thomas Bateman in the mid-nineteenth century and, with the absence of Global positioning systems or advanced survey techniques at that time, we have to work out from his descriptions which was which.

Bateman described the first barrow he dug as being in a small plantation. The account in 'Vestiges of the antiquities of Derbyshire' lists four burials. A crouched inhumation was placed in a cist together with a food vessel (this refers to a style of decorated pot often found with burials – it should not imply that the dead were laid to rest with their cooking pots!). The cremated remains of two children were accompanied by a food vessel and a further skeleton buried with a pygmy cup – a small vessel with an open lattice design – was found higher up in the mound. The second location of two adjacent barrows was, according to Bateman, on a ridge overlooking Alsop and this, descriptively at least, fits the mound further along the wall to the left, amongst the trees on the hilltop! Again there were inhumations and cremations of adults and children but, in addition, Bateman describes iron rivets amongst the grave goods. If he is right, this would imply a later date.

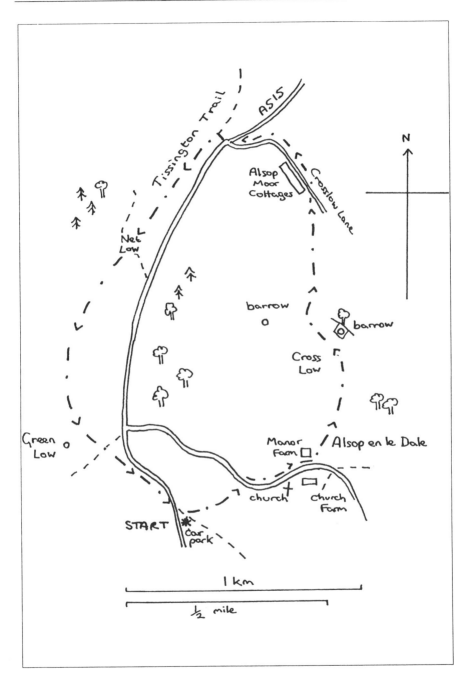

Continue over the brow of the hill, following the path to the left, around the corner of a field. Turn right, staying adjacent to the wall, and you come to the next stile. The way now veers to the left slightly, crossing three more fields and emerging onto a lane just to the right of the row of cottages you can see ahead. Turn left into Crosslow Lane and this brings you out onto the A515.

Cross the road and straight ahead is the Tissington Trail. If you look to the north along the trail, you can see the distinctive tree-capped peak of Johnson's Knoll. Just to the left of this, on the slightly lower hillside beyond, is the location of Liff's Low. This Neolithic cairn was first excavated by Bateman in 1843 and has been the subject of further investigations this century. Bateman's strategy was to tunnel into the centre of the mounds on the assumption that here would be located the primary burial with its associated grave goods. After spending perhaps half a day on one barrow he would move on to another site. In this case he found a limestone cist containing a crouched skeleton together with goods including a pot, two flint axes, boar's tusks and arrowheads, an antler macehead, some red ochre and other flint tools. However, an excavation nearly a hundred years later revealed a skeleton with a beaker and stone pendant (reconstructed in Buxton museum) and three further skeletons. The idea that a barrow was constructed for one high-ranking individual has had to be rethought.

Turn left onto the Tissington Trail. After just a few metres is the location of Net Low (or Nettly Knowe) where, in 1845, Bateman excavated an extended skeleton. The jaw of the individual had been placed by his feet and beside him was a bronze dagger and two jet buttons.

Continue along the path for almost half a mile. Just before the track turns to go under a bridge, Green Low is located just behind the field wall a hundred metres to your right. You can get a better look by taking the path in the next field and doubling back to look over the wall (remember you are now on private land). Green Low is an important Beaker burial and like Liff's Low has been the subject of several excavations. The crouched skeletons of a man and child were found, together with a beaker, a flint dagger and several smaller

The beaker from Green Low barrow, near Alsop

artefacts such as arrowheads, bone tools and pieces of iron pyrites (fool's gold).

At least two other barrows are known to have existed between Net Low and Green Low but it is likely that they were destroyed with the building of the railway. In their prime they would have been roughly in alignment, probably each one visible from the next.

It is now less than half a mile down the Tissington Trail back to the car park.

Finding out more:

Bateman, T 1848 *Vestiges of the antiquities of Derbyshire* (Smith)

Fowler M J & J W Corcoran 1955 'The transition from Late Neolithic to Early Bronze Age in the Peak District of Derbyshire & Staffordshire' *DAJ*

Walk 5: Wigber Low and Bradbourne

Distance: 4½ miles (7km)

Starting Point: SK207503. Park your car in Kniveton village.

Refreshments: There is a pub in Kniveton.

Alternative Routes: This walk can be combined with Walk 6 for a longer route by taking a footpath north from Bradbourne towards Rainster Rocks and returning from Harborough Rocks via Hognaston.

Preamble

Wigber Low is a multi-phase barrow, used from Neolithic to Anglo-Saxon times, while Bradbourne boasts a church with Norman and Saxon stonework. This is a comparatively short walk but it can be surprisingly strenuous crossing the fields and climbing the hills in damp conditions – prepare to get muddy. The first half of the route is accessed by particularly narrow gates, favouring the more slender walker!

The Walk

Take the track on the left of the Red Lion pub, a potentially muddy route, it winds its way up the hill between walls and hedges. Ignore the marked footpath across fields to the left and continue along the main path, passing through a narrow gate on your right, then turning immediately left to follow the field boundary. After about half a mile you come to a lane which you should cross and take the footpath on the opposite side.

As you walk across the fields you can see Wigber Low – the rather lumpy hill straight ahead. Beyond this, to the right, you can see the distinctive conical tree-capped hill of Minning Low in the distance. The way passes Longrose farm; keep the farm buildings to your left, after which you have a choice of going straight ahead through the gate towards Wigber Low or striking a little to the left where the now-familiar narrow gates lead across lower ground to the west of the hill. The paths converge again after half a mile and the more easterly route is preferable if you want a closer look at Wigber Low.

Where the hill forms a distinctive promontory to the north, a pile of stones marks the remains of a cairn. Wigber Low has been excavated several times and gradually its complex history has been revealed. Archaeologists believe that the hilltop was first used in the Neolithic between 5000-6000 years ago, when it was an exposure platform for the dead. There are several reasons for thinking this. Firstly, burials or depositions of bones at that time were almost always disarticulated (the bones were separate and often not in the configuration of a human skeleton) and it is clear that the dead were excarnated (defleshed), probably pecked by birds on high platforms, before the bones were placed in tombs. At Wigber Low, small bones such as fingers were found to have fallen between the rocks, suggesting that the location may have been used for this purpose. With Minning Low clearly visible in the distance, it is interesting to speculate whether the bones defleshed at Wigber were later deposited in the tombs on Minning Low, perhaps being carried along a ceremonial pathway between the two.

In the Bronze Age, the platform on Wigber Low was enlarged into a barrow. This time it was intended as a final resting place for the burials. However, the story does not end there. Over 2000 years later, in the seventh century AD, the mound was reused for Anglo-Saxon burials.

Continue north along the path – it runs on the right-hand side of the field wall with Wigber Low rising up on your right. The route joins up with the driveway from a building on your left. Follow this rather steep and stony track down to the road. Turn right, passing the stream and mill buildings then turn right onto the signposted footpath across the fields. This leads you into the village of Bradbourne (about one third of a mile).

Pause in Bradbourne to look at the church. Just inside the churchyard, approaching through the gate next to the vicarage, is the shaft of a ninth century Anglo-Saxon cross. The church itself has some fine carving over a Norman arch and if you go round the back and look at the north wall of the nave there are remnants of Anglo-Saxon stonework. Christianity arrived in Britain in the seventh century

A Norman archway in Bradbourne church

with the immigrant Angles and Saxons soon adopting it. It is strange to think that the descendants of the people buried in Wigber Low may have built the first Saxon church in Bradbourne.

Return to the main road and walk due east, taking the lane on the right towards Hognaston. After half a mile, a track curves up the hillside to the right, cutting between Haven Hill on the right and Bank Top on the left. The shortest route back is to follow this up the hill where it is joined by a trackway from Banktop Farm. A more substantial route now leads down via Newhouse Farm, arriving on the main street of Kniveton near to the church. Alternatively, continue a few hundred yards further along the road and take the path across the footbridge to the right. Walk across the fields, past the farm buildings, until you come to a road. Turn right along the road into Kniveton.

Finding out more:

Bunting, Richard 1993 *Anglo-Saxon and Viking Derbyshire* J H Hall & Sons, Derby.

Collis J 1983 *Wigber Low, Derbyshire: A Bronze Age and Anglian burial site in the White Peak* (University of Sheffield)

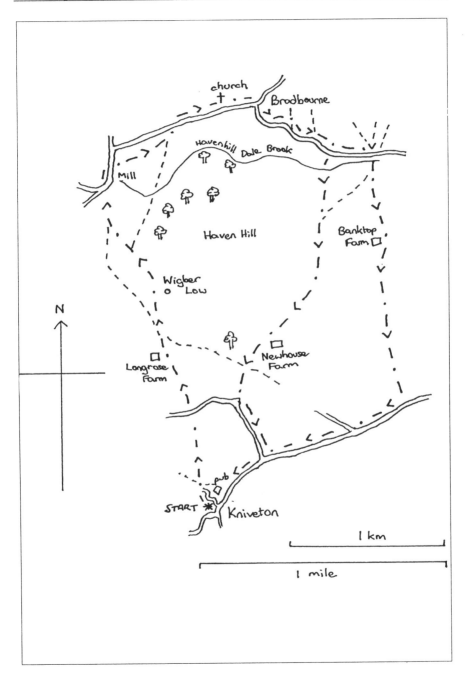

Walk 6: Rainster Rocks and Harborough Rocks

Distance: 5½ miles (9km)

Starting Point: SK230544. Park your car in Brassington village.

Refreshments: There are several pubs in Brassington and at time of writing the village shop was open each morning from 9.00 – 1.00. The station shop at Longcliffe also advertises snacks.

Preamble

Two rocky outcrops are featured on this walk. At Rainster Rocks you can see the roadway and enclosures of a Romano-British settlement, while at Harborough you can visit the site where Iron age people made their home. This is a fairly easy stroll, much of it on level ground.

The Walk

From the main street, go through the gate on the far left of the churchyard and follow the wall on your left until you come out onto a narrow lane. Turn left and after a few metres there are two ways into the field on your right, an unmarked stile almost immediately or a signposted path a little further along the lane. Once in the field, bear left and climb up the hill, striking north of the wall on your left to cross a stile into the next field. Then turn half-right and you should come out at the end of a farm lane. Ignore the footpath opposite and instead turn left down this lane, taking the signposted footpath on your right after the next field wall.

You can now see the outcrop of Rainster Rocks ahead and should head in this direction, passing covered shafts amongst the mine workings in the field. You will cross a path that winds through the field and the stile over the next wall is just to the right of the small rocky outcrop directly ahead. From here, a post marks the track of the footpath both straight ahead and from north to south. For now your way lies ahead but later you will need to return to this post to continue with the walk.

Carry on towards the rocks but as the path begins to climb you should skirt round to the left to the south-east base of the first major outcrop. This is the site of a Romano-British settlement and if you look carefully you should be able to make out enclosure walls in the earthworks with a roadway running between them.

In Roman times, lead was formed into ingots known as pigs and in Derbyshire these were stamped with the letters LVT, LVTVD or LVTVDARES. These distinguishing codes are believed to refer to Lutudarum, a 'lost' administration centre for Peak District lead mining which, some historians believe, was located at Rainster Rocks. However, there are also good arguments that it could have been sited in several other places such as Wirksworth or Cromford.

The Romano-British settlement at Rainster Rocks – see accompanying text

Return to the post marking the footpath and this time head north across the field. Soon another path joins from the right and the way ahead continues on the west side of the wall. Follow this field boundary until you reach the road, then turn right. After a little less than half a mile, the High Peak Trail crosses the road on the bridge. You can either scramble up the embankment on the left or walk under the bridge to Longcliffe and turn right onto the footpath.

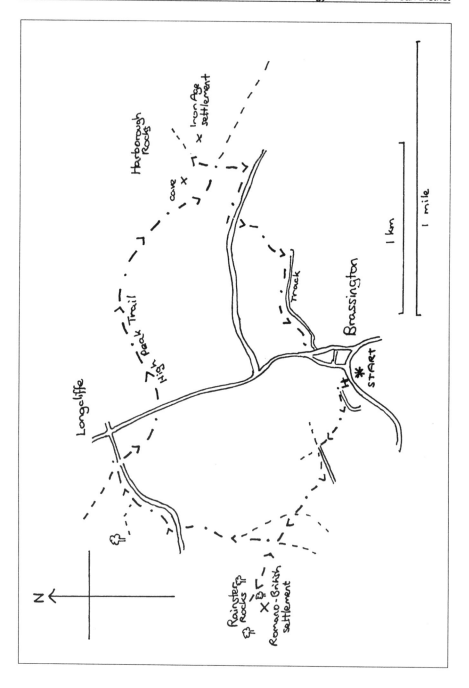

Heading south-east on the course of the disused railway, Rain's Cave is situated in the hillside to your right. The entrance is not accessible but the cave was excavated in the late nineteenth century by Ward, who found seven skeletons of Neolithic date. At least one of the skulls he excavated was described as dolichocephalic, this means it was narrow in shape, typical of those found early in the Neolithic; later, about the time of the arrival of the Beaker culture, human skulls changed to a brachycephalic or wider shape. At first this change was interpreted as an invasion and domination by European immigrants. Today, it is recognised that such change could come about from a comparatively small and peaceable genetic input or because of outside factors such as diet.

It is a mile and a half to Harborough Rocks, the distinctive hill and limestone outcrop on the left. As you approach, you can see Harborough Cave halfway up the terraces.

At the brickworks, footpaths are signposted to the left and right. Take the turning to the left and make your way up the path, bearing left to the cave. Several artefacts were found here including a

The Chair on top of Harborough Rocks. A chambered tomb once stood in front of the present-day trig point

coral-mounted bronze brooch, a bronze pin, two iron spearheads, a fragment of shale bracelet and pottery dating to the Early Iron Age and before. Turn and walk to the southern end of the same terrace. This area and the corresponding ledge above appear to have been the main centre of activity of the Iron Age community. Considerable amounts of pottery were found here and, on the higher platform, it is possible that dips in the ground formed the bases of house platforms.

Now make your way up to the top. There is a distinctive rock called the 'chair' for obvious reasons and further along the hilltop is the Ordnance Survey triangulation point. Between these two features is the site of a Neolithic tomb – now sadly destroyed. It once took the form of a passage grave, similar to those that at Five Wells, Minning Low and Green Low, Aldwark. A single internal chamber was excavated by Ward and found to contain at least sixteen skeletons and three leaf-shaped arrowheads. Six of the skeletons were in a crouched position, which suggests a Later Neolithic date – perhaps 2500BC. Of the others, it is difficult to tell whether they had been excarnated before burial, which would suggest an Earlier Neolithic date, or whether the burials had simply been disturbed.

Retrace your steps back down the path to the High Peak Trail and take the marked path opposite. Turn right onto Manystones Lane then left onto the footpath signposted after about a quarter of a mile. The path follows the field boundary on the left and bends to the right and left before emerging onto the end of a tarmacked lane. In fact this is a farm track so the only traffic you are likely to encounter is a tractor. Turn right into this lane and it brings you into the north of Brassington.

Finding out more:

Brailsford J W 1957 'Later prehistoric cave dwellings of Derbyshire' *DAJ*

Dool J 1976 'Roman material from Rainster Rocks, Brassington' *DAJ*

Ford D & J Rieuwerts (eds) 1968 *Lead Mining in the Peak District* (Peak Park)

Makepeace G A 1990 'An early Iron Age settlement at Harborough Rocks, Brassington' *DAJ*

Monet-Lane H C 1986 *The Romans in Derbyshire: Lead mining and the search for Lutudarum* (Veritas, Derbyshire)

Walk 7: Minning Low and Roystone Grange

Distance: 5 miles (8km)

Starting Point: Minning Low car park SK194582. Park at Minning Low car park, this is located on the road from Pikehall to Parwich, approximately 1km south of the A5012.

Refreshments: There are no cafes or pubs on the route so take food and drink with you. For after the walk, there are pubs at Parwich and Grangemill and a tea shop at Elton.

Alternative Routes: Those favouring a longer walk may prefer to link this route with Walk 8 by continuing south-east down the High Peak Trail towards Longcliffe and branching left to Slipper Low farm. After visiting Green Low and Stoney Low, turn right onto the road and there is a track on the left, immediately after Rockhurst Farm, which emerges onto the road just north of Minninglow car park.

Preamble

Minning Low is a stunning place both visually and archaeologically. The conical tree-capped hill is a distinctive landmark and can be seen for a considerable distance from most directions. Close up, the large complex of Neolithic chambered tombs are partially back-filled, their huge capstones and supporting slabs having stood there for 5000 years. The monastic farm of Roystone Grange dates to medieval times and a small section of the original buildings can still be seen; in addition, a Romano-British settlement is buried within its enclosures. This walk follows much of the Roystone Grange trail, however, I prefer to take the opposite direction to the yellow markers as this gives a more majestic approach to Minning Low and the opportunity to continue the walk to Green Low. The route is comfortable walking for people of all levels of fitness.

The Walk

From the car park, continue down the road towards Parwich for about a quarter of a mile. At the first crossroads turn left. You are now facing Minning Low, the round, tree-capped hill which dominates the landscape. Follow this road for a further quarter of a mile and bear right at the bend to pass Roystone Cottages (a track continues straight ahead, a possible return route).

Carry on between the hills. You may notice at least one quarried area to your left. For the next km, on the ridge to your left you can see a succession of humps and bumps. These are barrows or burial mounds dating to the early Bronze Age. They are so prolific that this stretch of hillside has been described as a Bronze Age cemetery.

Two Romano-British settlements have been identified at Roystone Grange. The first begins just north of the present day farm and extends to the south for about half a mile. It comprises several buildings and walled enclosures, in particular a probable farm building, sometimes described as a proto-villa, which began as a timber-framed, aisled hall and was later rebuilt in stone. Two skeletons were found in this area implying a small cemetery. There was also evidence of lead smelting. A little way down the track to the right, south of the farm, is the lead rake which provided the raw material. It is thought, from the style of the architecture, that the people living here between 200 – 400AD were descendants of Iron Age farmers from further south in the Midlands. Field systems on the hillside to the east are also attributed to these people.

Continue down the main track and you will soon come to a chapel-like building. This is a 19th century pumping house which supplied power for the construction of the railway which, now dismantled, forms the High Peak Trail.

You are now standing amidst the remains of the buildings of Roystone Grange. This monastic farm was given to the Cistercian abbey of Garendon in Leicestershire during the 12th century. For the next 200 years, sheep were tended here by lay brethren. To the west of the pumping house you can see the remains of a hall and barn. Pottery found here suggests that this area was probably a dairy. Further buildings lie buried a few metres to the north. An information

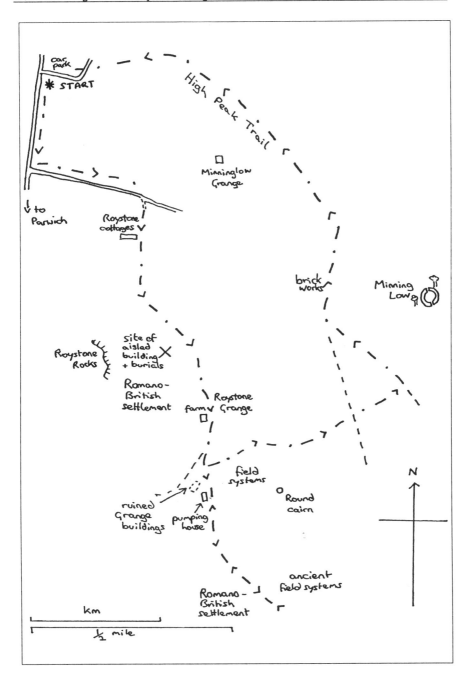

board on the wall of the pumping house gives information on the grange and nearby ruins.

You may wish to take a further detour by following the main track a little further to the south. In the fields to your right lie the remains of the second Romano-British settlement. This is thought to be either of lower economic status than the more northerly buildings or of later occupation.

On the hillside to the left are more ancient field systems, their date is unknown but they are probably part of the settlement opposite.

Walk back towards the present day farm and take the footpath signposted to the right just north of the pumping house. Follow this uphill across the fields.

On the hillside around here are several Bronze Age barrows. On the hill to your right is the Roystone Grange round cairn. When this was excavated, burials of at least seven individuals were found, often accompanied by a pot or urn (when pots were first used to accompany burials it was customary for the pot to be placed beside the body rather than to contain a cremation or inhumation). Of these, three were cremated and of the others, one was buried in a crouched position and another in an extended (lying) position. This shows that this was a final resting place rather than a temporary repository. A further barrow nearby was found to have been excavated at least twice in the nineteenth century and contained similar remains.

Half way up the hill is a stile on your left. If you pause before climbing into the next field and look at the hillside a few metres away on your right, you may be able to make out the remains of Romano-British field walls.

Cross the stile but keep to the right, continuing up the hill. Soon the path passes under an archway of the High Peak Trail. You will soon come to the grassy walled track that forms part of the Roystone Grange Trail. From here, Minning Low chambered tombs are just a few minutes walk up the hill. There are no official footpaths but the intervening land is open pasture and a visit to the site is a must. You should, nonetheless, obtain permission from the landowner. The perimeter is fenced to protect recently planted trees but there are entrances to the inner burial area to the north-west and south-east.

The Minning Low tombs have been excavated on several occasions, by Thomas Bateman in the mid-nineteenth century and again by Barry Marsden in 1974. During these explorations, four chambered tombs have been identified and it is possible that still more are waiting to be discovered. They date to the Neolithic so they were built and used before the barrows on the hillside above Roystone Grange. We cannot be sure if they were regarded as separate and individually covered with mounds of stones or whether the area was effectively one monument, eventually covered by a huge cairn. However, it is generally accepted that chamber 1 was the first to be built.

The various remains of bone and pottery uncovered show that the area was used over a long period of time, perhaps for several centuries, certainly into the early Bronze Age. Although only fragments of human bones were found, we must presume that the stone chambers originally contained many human remains. From what we know of similar monuments, it is likely that the individuals interred here were defleshed and stored as a communal collection of bones,

The distinctive hill of Minning Low

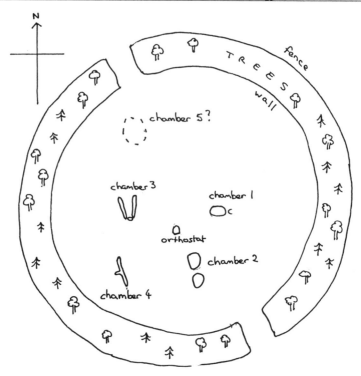

The chambered tomb complex on Minning Low

perhaps for use in ceremonies and to mark the territory of their descendants. Sadly, the excavated chambers have had to be backfilled due to vandalism but you can still see some of the supporting portals and covering capstones and the area is well worth close inspection.

Minning Low has paid the price for occupying such a prime position. The first to come looting were the Romans (a Roman road passes just a few hundred metres away), betraying their presence with coins and fragments of their pottery scattered within the chambers. It is likely that more robbing expeditions have taken place since, both in the hope of finding grave goods and for the stones which formed the covering cairns and which today probably form parts of the drystone walls in the vicinity.

When you have finished exploring Minning Low, return to the grassy lane you crossed earlier.

Walk north-west along the lane and you will soon arrive at the junction with the High Peak Trail. This is the site of Minning Low brickworks where, in the second half of the nineteenth century, bricks were produced to build the embankment and viaduct for the railway.

From here you can either take the track opposite, which brings you back to the road near Roystone Grange cottages, or turn right and walk along the High Peak Trail which leads directly into the car park.

Finding out more:

Hodges R & M Wildgoose 1981 'Roman or native in the White Peak: The Roystone Grange Project & its regional implications' *DAJ*

Hodges R, J Thomas & M Wildgoose 1989 'The barrow cemetery at Roystone Grange' *DAJ*

Hodges R & M Wildgoose 1991 'Roystone Grange: excavations of the Cistercian grange 1980-87' *DAJ*

Marsden B 1982 'Excavations at the Minning Low chambered cairn, Ballidon, Derbyshire' *DAJ*

Probert S 1988 'Excavations at the Minning Low brickworks' *DAJ*

Walk 8: Green Low

Distance: 4 miles (7km)

Starting Point: Aldwark, (SK228573). Park in the centre of Aldwark by the small green.

Refreshments: There are no refreshments on route but after the walk you may wish to visit the pubs at Grangemill or Parwich or the tea shop at Elton.

Alternative routes: For a longer walk you can link with the Minning Low route — see Walk 7.

Preamble

There are two sites in this book called Green Low, this one is a chambered tomb dating to the end of the Neolithic or Early Bronze Age. The remains of another burial site at Stoney Low are also visited. This is a relatively short and gentle route, the only potential hazard being a rather marshy area in a field.

The Walk

Follow the road that curves north west towards Elton and take the footpath marked to the right immediately after Lidgate farm. After crossing several fields, you come to a stile at the top of the ridge. This will be your way ahead later. However, to visit Green Low chambered tomb, you need to go through the gate on your right and walk a few hundred metres due east. Please note, this is private land.

The Green Low Passage Grave is located near the top of the ridge on the northern edge of the hill, with a quarried area to the north east and sloping grassy pasture to the south. You can still see the upper part of the stone slabs, the more northerly 'room' is the burial chamber and the southern enclosure is the entrance passage. On either side of the entrance are the remains of a stone facade. The archaeological evidence suggests that this monument was built in the Later

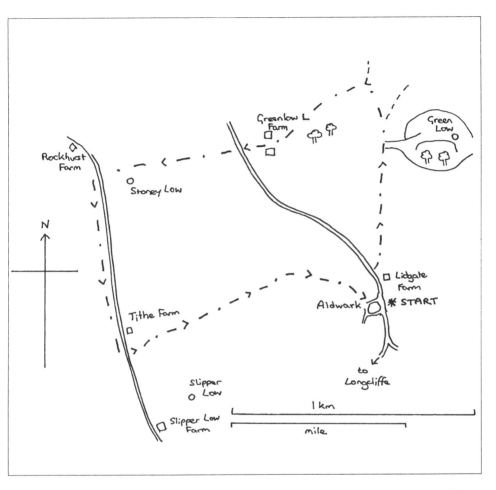

Neolithic and, like Minning Low, would probably have contained the bones of previously defleshed individuals. When their use was finally over the entrance area was filled in.

Although, like Minning Low, Green Low was disturbed in Romano-British times there is still plenty to be learned from the site. A complete skeleton was found to the east of the chamber and the repository itself contained further human bones together with those of sheep and oxen. The surrounding cairn material contained sherds of early Beaker pottery (typically found at the end of the Neolithic) and more bones – human, pig, dog, sheep and red deer.

The remains of the chambered tomb at Green Low

Return to the main path and cross the stile to the north. The original route of the right of way is a little unclear because field walls have been removed but essentially you need to skirt around the north side of the wooded hill to your left and join a path leading to Greenlow farm. Once there, follow the farm track out to the road. Cross the road and take the grassy path flanked by stone walls, almost opposite.

Towards the end of this path, as you approach a further road, you will pass Stoney Low on your left. This large passage grave was destroyed for road building but originally contained several cists housing skeletons, an urn cremation and 161 human teeth. There is sadly now little to see of this monument but you may be able to identify a circle of stones marking the perimeter of the cairn. It is also interesting to note that two stone circles were reported nearby in the 19th century but there is no trace of either now.

When you reach the road turn left (unless you are returning to Minninglow car park, in which case you should turn right, then left after the farm). Follow the road for a third of a mile passing Tithe

Farm on your left. After the farm are some cottages and immediately after these is a footpath. Follow this path to the left, it starts as a well-established track that leads to a stile beyond the buildings. Cross the stile and begin to climb the slope. To your right you can see a hill immediately behind a farm (Slipper Low), this is the site of a barrow excavated in the nineteenth century. Within a rock-cut grave were found a Beaker (the distinctive decorated pottery of the early Bronze Age – often accompanying burials) and several disturbed inhumations and cremations. Recent field-walking at the farm has produced small flint blades, these are are thought to date to the late Mesolithic (6000-8000 years ago) and were probably combined to form composite tools.

Carry on up the hill. There are a few hazards on this path including marshy ground and electric fences but you will eventually come to a stile in a stone wall. Cross the stile and turn immediately left through a gate. Bear right and follow the contour of the hill. The path is not always obvious but if you keep a few metres down from the distinctive rocky outcrop which soon appears on your right, you will not get lost.

The path eventually leads down to Aldwark, bearing right to emerge near the Coach house and green.

Finding out more:.

Manby T G 1958 'Chambered tombs of Derbyshire' *DAJ*
Manby T G 1965 'The excavation of Green Low Chambered Tomb' *DAJ*
Slipper Low – DAJ 1996

Walk 9: Arbor Low and Ringham Low

Distance: 9 miles (14km).

Starting Point: Monyash, SK150667. Monyash is signposted a mile to the east of the A515 Ashbourne – Buxton road. Leave your car in the parking area opposite the Methodist church.

Refreshments: There is a tea shop in Monyash but take a picnic as there is no food or drink available during the walk.

Preamble

This is a circular route visiting the chambered tomb of Ringham Low to the north of Lathkill Dale and the henge and stone circle of Arbor Low, the best known of the Peak District prehistoric monuments, to the south. The route to Arbor Low necessitates a detour of about one mile, part of which is on a road. Unfortunately, this is unavoidable as no public footpaths go near to the site. Those walking with children may prefer to omit this detour and drive directly to Arbor Low afterwards.

The Walk

From the Methodist church, walk northwards up the road. After a few hundred metres you will leave the village behind. Take the right hand fork (Horse Lane) and turn almost immediately right onto the marked footpath. You are now in Bagshaw Dale. Follow the path across the fields, crossing the Bakewell road after about half a mile, this leads you into Lathkill Dale.

Various paths, some marked and some unofficial, branch off on either side, you should keep to the track at the bottom of the valley. The flanking hillsides become rocky and steep (the entrance to the first of the disused mines lies to the right), and soon you will pass scree slopes of quarried rocks and boulders on your left. This is some

Arbor Low stone circle and henge – a barrow is sited on top of the bank
in the background

of the waste from the now disused Ricklow quarry. Immediately after this, and half a mile from the road, is a wall with a stile. Turn left just before the wall and climb the steep rock-cut steps up the hillside. You will soon reach a platform where the steps continue abutting the wall and a path branches off to the left, follow this path through Ricklow quarry.

The path bends to the right around the hilltop and leads through a gate into pasture fields. Continue to follow this route to the north, with a stone wall on your left until you come to a sign marking a footpath 'crossroads' (from here you can see a road two fields away; if you have reached the road then you've gone too far!). Take the path to the right and make your away across the fields, you should be walking due east, parallel with Lathkill Dale.

In an otherwise treeless landscape, there are two clumps of trees downhill to your right. In the second of these is the chambered tomb of Ringham Low. Much of the original covering mound has now been destroyed, there is just a slightly raised area north of the wall and in the plantation to the south you can see the remains of a robber trench. Although it does not look a very impressive place today, when it was built, probably during the Neolithic, Ringham Low would have been a very important place. It is likely that the bodies deposited here were first excarnated, that is to say defleshed, probably by being placed on high platforms to be pecked by birds. After weeks or months, the clean bones would have been placed in the tomb. Original excavation reports indicated that the remains of at least thirteen individuals were placed here.

From Ringham Low go back up the field to the stile and continue on the path which, after the next wall, swings down to the right crossing the next two fields diagonally. The route is a little hard to find just here. In fact the path turns to the left, seemingly the wrong direction, and crosses a stile in the top corner into a paddock surrounded by trees and hedges. You should then turn right and a stile at the southern end of the enclosure leads the way on. The way down into Lathkill Dale is now more obvious and after two more fields a gate with an information board gives access to a steep path down.

You have now come to the River Lathkill. Lathkill Head Cave is half a mile to the right on the opposite bank while to the left the river becomes canalised and passes various mine adits. However, your path lies straight ahead, across the footbridge and up Cales Dale.

Climbing up to the west of Cales Dale, you come to One Ash Grange Farm. As its name may suggest, it was originally a grange or monastic farm. Many such farms existed in the Peak District between the 12th and 14th centuries, most were owned by Cistercian abbeys and were sheep farms run by lay brethren. Later, some continued under the same administration, while others were leased out to tenants. The grange at One Ash was originally located a little to the south-west and the farm buildings were moved to the present site probably during the sixteenth century. Another grange is situated at Calling Low, half a mile to the south-east.

After passing the main farm buildings, take the concessionary path signposted to Cales Farm. The hillside to your right is the site of One Ash village, a settlement that pre-dates the original grange and is mentioned in the Domesday Book.

From Cales Farm, continue along the track towards the road,

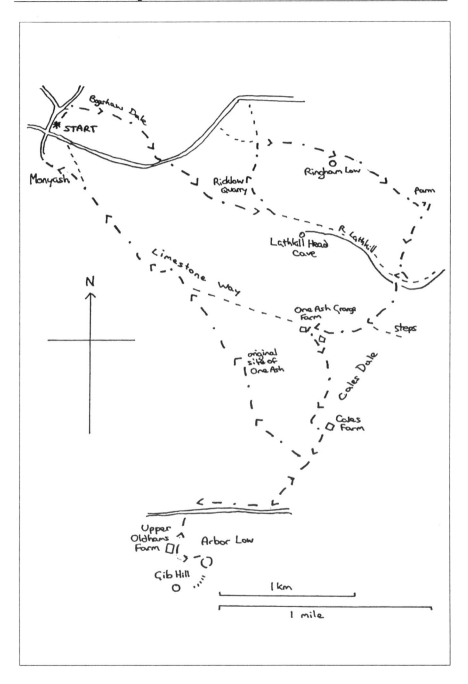

N

Bagshaw Dale

* START

Monyash

Ricklow Quarry

Ringham Low

farm

R. Lathkill

Lathkill Head Cave

Limestone Way

One Ash Grange Farm

steps

Coles Dale

original site of One Ash

Coles Farm

Upper Oldhams Farm

Arbor Low

Gib Hill

1 km

1 mile

crossing one field. An unmarked footpath runs along the south side of the wall bounding this field and this will be your route after visiting Arbor Low. Turn right onto the road and, after a few hundred metres, Arbor Low is signposted on the left. Follow the footpath, walking through the henge and out through the south entrance.

Gib Hill is the large mound across the field. It is likely that in prehistory, before erosion and excavation, it was much bigger than it is today. It is perhaps better described as a man-made hill than as a barrow (the latter tends to imply that the primary function is for burial) and it is often compared with Silbury Hill at Avebury in Wiltshire. Gib Hill was built sometime in the Neolithic, certainly before the bank and ditch of the henge were dug. It is common, however, for Neolithic monuments to contain some human remains even though they may not be regarded as burial sites and archaeologists usually interpret such deposits as expressing a presence, perhaps claiming rights over territory. Gib Hill is no exception, containing layers of burnt bone – both human and animal. Like the bank of the henge, it also has a later Bronze Age barrow built on top. This can be more literally regarded as a tomb and originally contained a burial in a stone cist.

Return to the henge and stone circle. It is common for people to confuse henges and stone circles, largely because of the most famous – Stonehenge – being known for its standing stones. In fact, a henge is a circular earthwork, usually comprising a bank with a ditch inside. It is also usual to have either just one entrance, or two roughly opposite one another; Arbor Low falls into the second category. Henges were commonly built in the Later Neolithic, around 2500BC and some, like Arbor Low, had stones added at a later date.

Arbor Low is referred to as a recumbent stone circle, that is to say the stones are lying down. There has long been a disagreement about whether the stones at Arbor Low ever stood but the current opinion of local archaeologists is that they did. There are several reasons for thinking this. Firstly, some of the stones are cracked or broken – presumably from when they fell. Secondly, the idea that they were never standing is partly based on the fact that there is no evidence of large pits where they were anchored in the earth. However, there is evidence of small pits and Peak District standing stones are commonly placed with the narrow end in the ground, requiring only a small amount of digging but resulting in many stones being unstable and either leaning or falling over.

The stones in the centre of the monument were originally arranged in a 'U' shape called a cove. A burial in the form of an extended inhumation was found in this area and was the subject of further controversy. It is usual to find burials at henges bent into a crouched or foetal position and therefore it was suggested the Arbor Low burial could have been deposited much more recently – perhaps during the last two hundred years! However, there are one or two similar examples in other parts of Britain and it is now thought to date to the Neolithic or Bronze Age. The skeleton was male and found with the skull broken into many pieces, several of the bones were missing including the lower jaw or mandible.

There is evidence of further burial in the form of a barrow on the bank adjacent to the southern entrance. You can still see a distinctive bump despite excavation and erosion. It has long been assumed that this monument was added after the building of the bank and indeed, excavation of its contents – burnt bones with Bronze Age urns – suggest a slightly later date than the henge. However, Bateman's excavation report states that the burial cist was placed on natural soil, i.e. the original ground surface, rather than the rubble of the bank. Perhaps the barrow existed here before or was contemporary with the henge.

It is now time to leave Arbor Low and return to Monyash, but before you go it is only fitting to make a gesture of respect to your ancestors. Human sacrifice is currently illegal so I suggest a picnic, not forgetting to pour a libation from your flask onto the ground!

There are no public footpaths passing Arbor Low so you will need to retrace your footsteps back past the farm and onto the road, turning right for almost half a mile then left on the path or track towards Cales Farm. At the far wall of the field crossed by pylons turn left, walking in a north-westerly direction along the south side of the wall. This is neither obvious nor signposted but it is marked as a right of way on the Ordnance Survey map. You will soon cross a shallow gully (the top of Cales Dale) and if you look up to the left here you can see Arbor Low on the hillside.

The path bears slightly more to the right now and passes the site of the original medieval One Ash Grange. The route continues in a north-westerly direction, cutting diagonally across the fields, until it joins the course of the Limestone Way, soon hooking to the left into a walled track. This well-trodden path leads you safely back into Monyash.

Finding out more:

Thompson, D 1963 *Official guide to Arbor Low* (Ministry of Works)

Rieuwerts, J 1973 *Lathkill Dale: its mines and miners* (Moorland)

Walk 10: Stanton Moor and Harthill Moor

Distance: 8½ miles (14km).

Starting Point: Birchover, SK238621. Park in the village of Birchover.

Refreshments: There are two pubs and a village store in Birchover. There is a pub at Stanton in Peak and about half way along the walk you can make a detour into Youlgreave where there are a number of pubs and cafes.

Alternative routes: This walk can be split into two shorter routes. Walk 10a (3½ miles) also starts at Birchover and visits Stanton Moor and Doll Tor stone circle. Walk 10b (3½ miles) starts in Youlgreave and visits Harthill Moor.

Preamble

This walk looks at some of the prehistoric remains on Stanton Moor. The best known of these is the Nine Ladies stone circle, which dates to the Bronze Age, but the path also passes other features such as burial cairns. There is a pleasant stroll through Stanton in Peak and Alport, then through meadows alongside the River Bradford. The route then joins the Limestone Way, deviating from it temporarily to visit the Iron Age hillfort of Castle Ring. Shortly after rejoining the Limestone Way, the Nine Stone Close circle can be seen from the path near the rocky outcrop of Robin Hood's Stride. This walk is particularly pleasant in July when the foxgloves are in flower and the bilberries are ripe on Stanton Moor.

The Walk

Walking north-east along the main street in Birchover, take the second footpath on the right, this is signposted 'Barn Farm'. Continue past the farm buildings and turn left at the footpath 'crossroads'. You will probably find tents in this field during the summer. When you

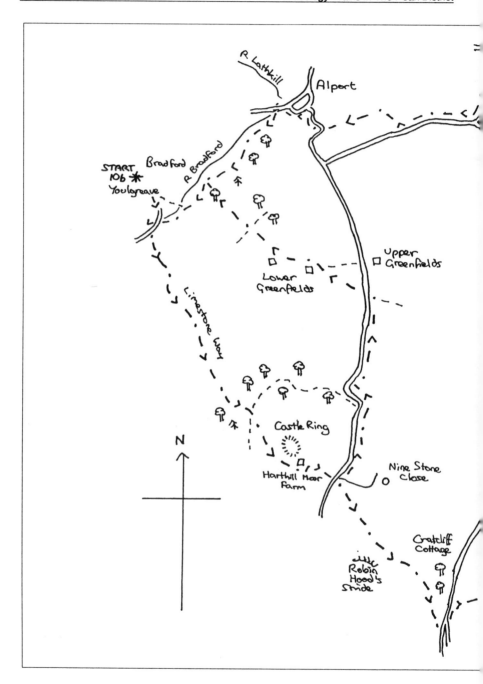

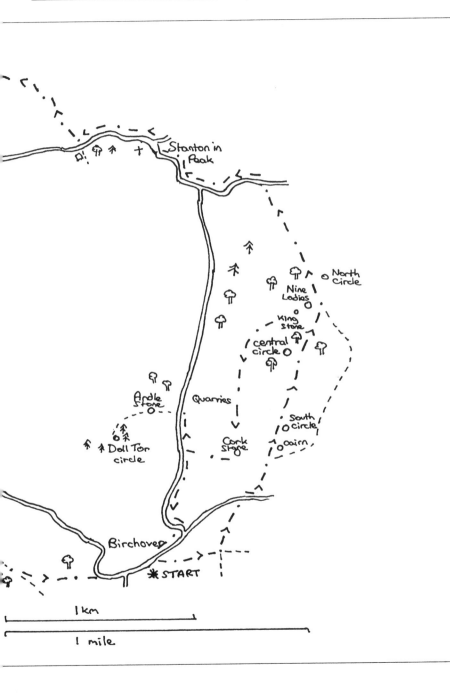

come to Lees Road the footpath continues over a stile on the far side of the road, a few metres to the right.

You are now on Stanton Moor. There are several routes passing manmade features and natural rock formations, you should follow the main path that leads straight ahead.

Stanton Moor is an area of highland formed by gritstone. There are dozens of prehistoric features, many of which have been excavated, and dating evidence suggests that they are all roughly contemporary, being built in the mid Bronze Age (about 1500 BC). The most well-known of the monuments are the stone circles, but besides these there are many burial mounds, largely obscured by undergrowth.

For some time, archaeologists have viewed such areas as a whole, describing them as sacred or ritual landscapes – even more specifically in the case of Stanton Moor as a Bronze Age cemetery. More recently though, archaeologists are recognising that the separation of religious and secular activity in today's western society is probably irrelevant to prehistoric life. Many believe that monuments such as stone circles may have had many functions and not just been reserved for the type of activity we would term ritual.

Stanton Moor is literally covered with archaeological features, most of them somewhat obscured by undergrowth. Just a few will be mentioned here but you will no doubt spot many more. As you climb up the hill, two paths branch off to the right. Midway between the second turning and the path 'crossroads' ahead, is a mound on the right hand side of the path. It is built of rubble with kerbstones around the edge. When excavated, the central pit was found to contain a cremated burial with a bronze knife.

Immediately after the crossroads, also on the right, is a second mound. This is the largest in the area and, although it is badly damaged, you may be able to locate a large outer ring of stones and a smaller inner one. In the centre, you can see the stone cist in which was found the main burial (usually termed the primary burial). Twelve other burials were found within the mound.

Continue northwards on the path. After about 150 metres you will come to the south circle, also on the right hand side. The bank, with its southern entrance, is clearly visible; it is revetted, inside and out with stone walling. The remains of a small stone circle lies inside the bank. This site has commanding views, both of the eastern moors and of impressive natural features such as the Gorse Stone and the Heart Stone to the east. Like this monument, most of the Peak District stone circles are embanked – that is they are surrounded by a circular rubble earthwork. This, combined with the fact that the stones in the Peak are usually quite small, can often make the circles difficult to spot, especially when they are overgrown with heather.

A further 400-500 metres on, a track to the left leads to the central circle (labelled on the O.S. map as an enclosure). This site has been classified both as a ringcairn and as an embanked stone circle. It appears similar in plan to the south circle, with a stone-walled bank, but is much larger and has entrances to the north and south, there are also indications of a flanking ditch. The interpretation of the site as a stone circle hinges on whether it ever had orthostats (apart from those at the entrances) or whether the many stones in its construction were simply part of the drystone walling. Both the central and south circles may have had central mounds but the ground is now too disturbed to be sure.

Return to the path and continue until you see the Nine Ladies stone circle on your left. At first sight, this appears to be one of the few complete and relatively undamaged stone circles in the Peak District, it does after all have nine stones set into a bank. But don't be fooled! It has sadly been damaged on many occasions and on one of these a tenth stone was unearthed. In addition, archaeologists suspect that an eleventh once stood. The circle has an outlier – the King Stone – situated a short distance to the south-west; such a feature is not unusual and occurs at stone circles in other parts of the country such as the Rollright Stones in Oxfordshire, which also boast a 'King Stone', and the Heel Stone at Stonehenge. There is little trace today of the bank that once surrounded the circle, or of the cairn in the centre.

➡ *Those following Walk 10a please turn to instructions for that route.*

After visiting the Nine Ladies, rejoin the main path and follow it

northwest. Just before you reach the first stone wall there is the remains of a further circle (the north circle) about 20 metres to the east
of the path but it is very overgrown and difficult to find.

Continue on the path until you rejoin Lees Road then turn left and
follow the main street through the village of Stanton in Peak, taking
the route towards Alport and Youlgreave. As you are leaving the village, take the footpath signposted on the right, immediately opposite
Stanton Lodge. After crossing a field, the path joins a trackway bending to the west, then crosses a further field before descending stone
steps to the road.

Turn left, walk along the road, and take the lane to the right. Immediately after Harthill Hall, on the right, there are several fields of
caravans. The right of way as depicted by Ordnance Survey is not
marked with a signpost but there are several gates including one
with an adjacent stile. Make your way to the far side of the caravan
park and the path becomes evident running alongside the rear wall.
Turn left onto this track and after a few minutes you will join the
lane into Alport. Cross the river and turn left. When you reach the
main road, turn left, then take the turning almost immediately on
the left, next to a telephone box; this starts as a wide driveway with a

The Nine Ladies stone circle

gate and is just a few metres north of the confluence of the rivers Lathkill and Bradford.

The next section of the walk is a particularly scenic stretch of riverside path. Follow the track across the river then along the south bank. You will pass a rocky outcrop, popular with climbers. If you are stopping for a picnic this is a good area, there is also a bench sheltered under the rock.

Continue beside the river until you come to a road. If you want to take a detour into Youlgreave for refreshments then cross the road and walk along the north-east riverbank, a path leads up to Youlgreave after a few hundred metres.

➡ *Those following Walk 10b join here.*

The way on is along the Limestone Way. It leads across fields due south from the road and is marked with a footpath sign. If you have come directly from Alport it is a left turn almost immediately after you have joined the road, a few metres after the farm track. You can now see the Iron Age hillfort of Castle Ring directly ahead. There are several hillforts in the Peak District and many others throughout the country. Chosen for their locations, which made them easily defen-

Castle Ring hillfort

sible, ramparts consisting of bank and ditch were built, enclosing an area on the top. At three-quarters of an acre, Castle Ring is very small but no less impressive.

Continue along the path towards Castle Ring, crossing stiles as necessary. Inside the field just below the hill, the path divides. The Limestone Way is signposted to the left and follows the contour of the hill to the northern side, you should take the path across the field, signposted to Robin Hood's Stride. Follow the waymarking posts up the hill, the marked path goes within metres of the summit. At the top, near to the modern field wall, you can see the defences comprising a bank, ditch and counter-scarp bank; the original entrance lies to the south-east.

Continue on the path past Harthill Farm. After the main farm buildings, the way is posted to the left and then to the right, following the drive down to the road. The Limestone Way rejoins at this point.

➡️ *Those following Walk 10b should now return to instructions for that route. If you wish to first make a detour to see Nine Stone Close, see the paragraph below.*

The footpath continues directly opposite, cutting diagonally across the field in a south-easterly direction to Robin Hood's Stride. Alternatively, to visit the Nine Stone Close circle, you must make a detour along the left hand wall of the field and the circle is just around the corner. Please note that this deviates slightly from the footpath and you should ask the landowner's permission first.

Nine Stone Close contains the largest stones of any Peak District circle, it is also unusual in that the stones are free-standing, there is no rubble bank surrounding them. Sadly only four stones remain in situ, but if you stand beside the circle and look towards Robin Hood's Stride you can see a fifth reused as a gatepost within the drystone wall.

Return to the footpath and continue past Robin Hood's Stride and the Hermit's Cave. When you come to the road, turn left for a short distance, then take the footpath on the right, up the hill. Bear left as the path levels out and continue around the north side of the hill on this contour. Keep straight ahead at the first junction then bear left at

Nine Stone Close with Robon Hood's Stride in the background

the fork and the path leads into Birchover, emerging (appropriately!) at one of the two pubs.

Finding out more:.

Barnatt J 1978 *Stone Circles of the Peak* (Turnstone, London).
Heathcote J P 1939 *The Nine Stones, Harthill Moor* DANHSJ Vol 8.
Heathcote J P 1954 *Excavations on Stanton Moor DANHSJ Vol 74.*
Preston, F 1954 'The hill-forts of the Peak' *DANHSJ* Vol 74

Walk 10a: Stanton Moor and Doll Tor Stone Circle

Distance: 3½ miles (5.5km).

Starting Point: Birchover village, SK238621.

Refreshments: Pubs and village store in Birchover.

Alternative Routes: To eliminate the walk to and from Birchover, park on the roadside on the Birchover – Stanton road and approach Stanton Moor via the Cork Stone.

Preamble

This walk is a pleasant stroll across Stanton Moor, with an optional detour to Doll Tor stone circle.

The Walk

➟*Follow directions for Walk 10 until indicated.*

Stanton Moor currently has unrestricted access and there are many small trackways not marked on official maps. Several of these will take you to the Cork Stone but this is the most direct route. From Nine Ladies, turn south-west and walk to the King stone. A path continues in the same direction, follow this until you come to a T-junction and then turn left. Paths branch off in various directions but you should take those which lead due south, keeping to the left of the quarried areas.

The Cork Stone is unmistakable, with iron staples set into the side to enable the more adventurous to reach the top and admire the view. Climbing this is an optional detour, not necessarily recommended! Turn right onto the well established path and this leads you to the Birchover-Stanton road.

From here, the Doll Tor stone circle is almost directly opposite, hidden in trees across the fields. To reach it, you should first turn

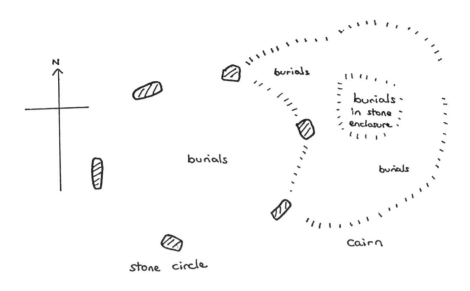

Doll Tor stone circle

right and walk along the road for a short distance until you are level with the Andle Stone – another unmistakable landmark very similar to the Cork Stone. Although there is no official right of way, the landowner allows access to the Andle Stone but please ask permission if possible. Cross the field to the stone then continue to the southernmost corner of the field beyond. A gate here leads to a track down the edge of a conifer plantation. At the point where the track bends to the right, the circle lies a few metres inside the woods to the left.

Doll Tor stone circle has an eventful history of excavation and vandalism. In the 1930s, excavations revealed a burial area, also dating to the Bronze Age, partially enclosing the circle. Grave goods included faience beads. Faience is an early form of glass manufactured in various shapes and colours and beads made from it are considered to be prestige items, indicating rich or powerful owners. It was originally thought to have been traded from Egypt but, more recently, archaeologists suspect it may have been produced in Britain.

Most recently, in the Spring of 1993, the Doll Tor circle was 'restored' by persons unknown. After their efforts, it comprised fourteen standing stones – a very generous reconstruction considering there were only six when it was first built! Following this event, local archaeologists did further excavations then attempted to restore the monument as closely as possible to its original plan. The resulting six stones are well worth a visit.

Retrace your steps via the Andle Stone then turn right onto the road and continue southwards back to Birchover.

Recent concerns and investigations on Stanton Moor

In 2000, Trent and Peak Archaeological Trust (T&PAT) conducted a survey, including limited excavation, to assess damage at the Nine Ladies stone circle. Erosion caused by the sheer number of visitors walking around the monument was found to be considerable (up to 5ins or 12cm). In addition, further damage had been caused by activities such as the lighting of campfires.

There is also continued debate and concern about whether quarrying will resume on Stanton Moor.

On a lighter note, while assessing damage to the Nine Ladies, Graeme Guilbert of T&PAT has drawn attention to the 'Bill Stumps' graffiti on the outlying stone known as the king and an almost identical quote in Charles Dickens' 'Pickwick Papers'. He explores the question of which came first in the DAJ (see below).

Finding out more:

Barnatt J 1997 'The excavation and restoration of Doll Tor stone circle, Stanton, Derbyshire 1994' *DAJ* Vol 117.

Guilbert, G 2001 'Foolishly inscribed but well connected – graffiti on the King, Stanton Moor' DAJ 121

Heathcote J P 1939 'Excavations at Doll Tor stone circle, Stanton Moor' *DANHSJ* Vol 8.

www.nottingham.ac.uk/tpau/projects/nls. Excavations at Nine Ladies for English Heritage, November 2000 (Trent and Peak Archaeological unit)

Walk 10b: Harthill Moor

Distance: 3½ miles (5.5km).

Starting Point: Youlgreave, SK270642. Park in Youlgreave.

Refreshments: Pubs and shops in Youlgreave. There is a "tea garden" down towards the river from the village hall.

Preamble

This walk follows the bank of the River Bradford then joins the Limestone Way to visit Castle Ring hillfort. There is an optional detour to Nine Stone Close stone circle before returning.

The Walk

Make your way south to the riverside and join the Limestone Way at the bridge, walking east along the north bank of the river. When you come to the road, turn right and follow it for a few metres before taking the path to the south (still the Limestone Way).

➥*Join Walk 10 where indicated.*

Turn left and follow the road north. This lane is usually quiet as regards vehicles but take care as it is narrow and winding. After a short distance there is a footpath through the trees on the left, this is the Limestone Way. If you want to return directly to Youlgreave you can take this route around the north side of Castle Ring and then retrace your steps across the fields, otherwise continue along the road for a further quarter of a mile.

The road soon straightens out and you leave the trees behind. A footpath crosses the road and you should take this route to the left through the marked gate. Continue across the fields, past Lower Greenfields farm, going straight ahead at the 'crossroads'. When you reach the river, turn left onto the path and continue until you come to the road. Join the Limestone Way on the far side of the road along the north bank of the river and take any of the right turns to lead you back into Youlgreave.

Walk 11: Crane's Fort and Conksbury

Distance: 7 miles (11km).

Starting Point: Youlgreave, SK209643. Park in the centre of Youlgreave.

Refreshments: Pubs, shops for ice creams and the like and a "tea garden" (down towards the river from the village hall) are located in Youlgreave. Refreshments are also available in Over Haddon and at Conksbury Farm.

Preamble

This walk forms a triangle, two sides of which are bounded by rivers. It is therefore particularly scenic and mostly on level ground. The route begins with a stroll along the River Bradford to Middleton to see the ruins of a castle and the tomb of the legendary Thomas Bateman, famous for a vast number of Peak District excavations in the 19th century. Then comes a hike cross country to look at Crane's Fort, an Iron Age structure. After crossing the river Lathkill there is an optional detour of about one mile to look at Mandale Mine and/or a detour into Over Haddon in search of refreshments. The route continues to the east down Lathkill Dale, crossing the bridge into Conksbury and the site of a medieval village.

The Walk

From the centre of Youlgreave, make your way down to the river, you can take one of several roads and pathways leading south from the main street. Having reached the River Bradford, cross via a footbridge to the opposite side and turn immediately right onto the path along the bank. This is part of the Limestone Way. There is now a pleasant stroll of a mile or so into Middleton. As you walk you may notice how the river is bricked into wide pools where it was once maintained as fishponds. After a mile, take the fork to the right signposted on the wall to Middleton.

The first stop is something of a pilgrimage. Turn right onto the road to the north and after a hundred metres, immediately after a building that was once a chapel, a gate on the left leads to Bateman's tomb. Although he only lived to be thirty-nine years old, Thomas Bateman was one of the most famous and prolific Derbyshire archaeologists. In the mid nineteenth century he excavated many barrows – he was known as the 'barrow-knight' – and, although his methods seem crude by today's standards, for his time he was meticulous in the way he described and recorded his work. Two books, 'Ten years diggings in Celtic and Anglo-Saxon grave mounds' and 'The vestiges of the antiquities of Derbyshire' give the accounts of his excavations.

Return to the road and cross to the eastern side. In the north-eastern corner of this field are the remains of Middleton Castle. Local tradition maintains that this limestone fortress was destroyed by shells fired by Cromwell's army during the Civil War.

Continue up the road. After half a mile, on a right-hand bend, take the footpath on the left across a field. Cross the road and continue north on the path opposite. This crosses several fields before crossing another road. This time the path turns half left, in line with the opposite field boundary and goes through a small wooded area and another field before coming to a road. Again the path is opposite, it bears right, crossing the fields diagonally to Meadow Place Grange.

Crane's Fort is a recently discovered hillfort dating to the Iron Age. It lies in the fields to the north-east of the farm buildings of Meadow Place Grange. Unfortunately there is no access into the fort although you may be lucky enough to gain permission to explore from the landowners – please do not cross the land otherwise. However, it is possible to see part of the fortifications. As you approach from the south-west, you can see the hillside of Crane's Fort in the middle distance and Over Haddon beyond. It is possible to see the bank marking the western boundary of the fort under the present day field wall. The enclosure extends across two fields to the east with the eastern boundary just outside the field wall on this side.

Continue across the fields to the farm and go through the farmyard as directed and across the field on the other side. In the far

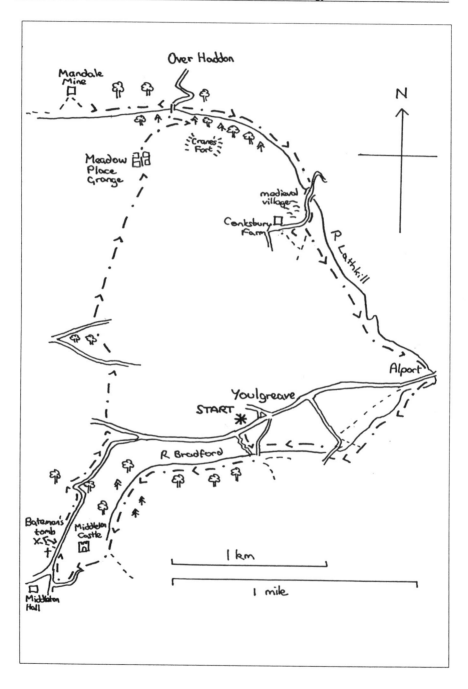

right-hand corner, a gate leads to the track down to Lathkill Dale. You can either look over the wall a few metres to the right of the gate or turn onto the track and scramble up the bank to your right. Again, you should be able to see the west bank of the fort by the far field wall. The fortifications comprise excavated limestone blocks with rubble infill, there is also a slight trace of an external ditch.

Continue down the track to the River Lathkill and cross the bridge. Fans of industrial archaeology may want to take a detour at this point to look at Mandale Mine which is located about five minutes walk away. If you do, turn left onto the marked riverside path and, after a quarter of a mile, look out for the track to the right. The bulk of the surface remains are hidden behind trees a few metres back from the river. The mine was worked from at least the 13th century, it was mentioned in 1288 in the Quo Warrento – an inquisition held in Ashbourne to look into Derbyshire miners' right to dig for lead ore. Part of the Cornish engine house can still be seen as can the pit that housed the 35ft (11 metre) diameter water wheel to the north-west of the Lodge Shaft. The base of a 9ft (2.7 metre) diameter

Mandale mine

chimney can be found on the hillside to the north-east. An entrance to the mine workings is protected by an iron grill but it is possible for enthusiasts to explore underground with a local caving or mining club.

Retrace your steps and continue east along the river bank. After a mile the path emerges onto the road at Conksbury Bridge. Cross the bridge and walk a hundred metres along the road. Pause here and look up to the fields on the right-hand side, you should be able to make out the earthworks of a deserted medieval village with a road-way winding from the bottom left-hand corner to the top right-hand corner of the field. It seems likely that the village was abandoned when the surrounding land came under monastic ownership and that the occupants went to live in Youlgreave.

The way ahead lies down the footpath to the left a few metres ahead. However, you may first wish to continue up the hill to Conksbury Farm where, at the time of writing, home-made tea and cakes are available on the front lawn.

Rejoin the path, now on the south-west side of the river. It is now one mile into Alport where you should cross the road and go down the driveway opposite to join the path along the River Bradford. When you reach the road at Bradford you should cross then rejoin the river on the north bank. You can now take any of the paths or lanes up into Youlgreave.

Finding out more:

Bateman T 1843 *Vestiges of the antiquities of Derbyshire* (Smith, London)

Bateman T 1861 *Ten years diggings in Celtic and Anglo-Saxon grave hills* (Smith, London)

Hart C R & G A Makepeace 1993 'Crane's Fort, Conksbury, Youlgreave, Derbyshire: A newly discovered hillfort' *DAJ*

Rieuwerts, J 1973 *Lathkill Dale: its mines and miners* (Moorland Publishing)

Walk 12: Fin Cop

Distance: 7½ miles (12km).

Starting Point: Parking area adjacent to the A6 (SK171706). The parking and picnic area is to the south-west of the A6, nearly three miles to the west of Ashford in the Water.

Refreshments: There are tea rooms and a pub at Monsal Head and similar amenities in Ashford.

Preamble

This walk explores the Iron Age hillfort of Fin Cop and benefits from the spectacular scenery of Monsal Dale and Monsal Head. An ancient settlement is also visited.

The Walk

From the car park, cross the road and follow the marked footpath opposite up Monsal Dale. Follow the river, you should pass a small waterwheel and a weir. The high peak up to your right is Fin Cop, this is the site of an Iron Age hillfort and you will have an opportunity to take a closer look at this later. After the weir, you will soon see a viaduct, across which, the Monsal Trail follows the path of the now dismantled railway. At this point you can either take the track up to the left onto the trail, turning right across the viaduct then following the path up the hill; alternatively you can continue under the arches, cross the river at the footbridge, then turn immediately right to climb to the top.

You are now at Monsal Head which is a good place to take a break and take advantage of the various amenities – and of course to admire the view.

At the front of the tea rooms, take the path signposted to Ashford, this initially leads south-west along the top of the ridge. After about half a mile the footpath to Ashford is signposted to the left. This will be your way on later. However, if you want to look at the fort then

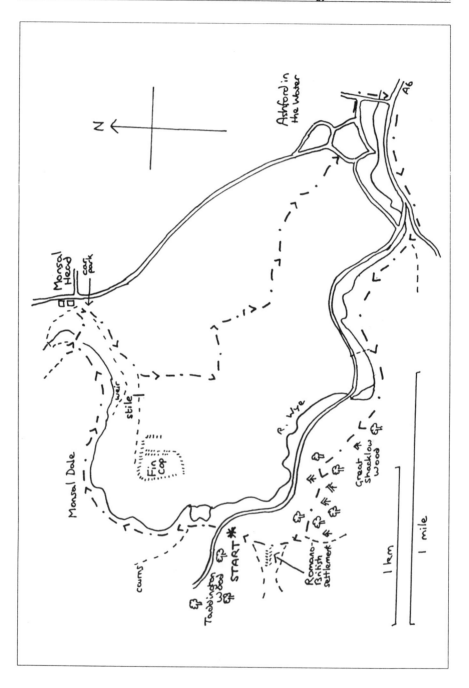

carry on straight ahead and a stile gives access to a track which runs round the top of the slope adjacent to a field wall on the left. Please note that the information I have received on access restrictions to this trackway is somewhat ambivalent and walkers going to view the fortifications must do so at their own risk, having said that, the bank and ditch ramparts are well worth seeing. I would emphasise, however, that no-one should go beyond the boundary of the fort; there is no way down the south of the hill and that area is policed by game-keepers protecting the trout in the river below.

At ten acres (four hectares), Fin Cop is one of the larger Peak District hillforts. The double bank and ditch fortifications, which can be viewed over the wall about a quarter of a mile along from the stile, are still very impressive despite the passage of time. You will notice that the inner bank – the second one you come to – is higher than the outer one, this is an obvious defensive design. This structure runs for two hundred and fifty metres with an entrance causeway half way along, it then turns to the south-west to join the west-facing precipice of the hill where only one bank and ditch are now visible.

The bank and ditch fortifications on Fin Cop

At both ends, the banks and ditches can be seen continuing beyond the wall. Even though they are much eroded, the ditch is still very evident because of the darker colour of the grass. When a ditch or hole is dug, in time it will fill up as weathering processes cause the surrounding material to slide or be blown into it. However, the new fill is likely to be composed of topsoil and humus in contrast to the rubble etc which was removed. Plants growing over such a feature now have a deep bed of nutrients for their roots and consequently the vegetational cover is lusher and taller, often darker in colour than the surrounding area. The patterns produced are known as positive crop marks.

Geographically, Fin Cop is very similar to Castle Naze although much larger. Both are sited on a high promontory, flanked on two sides by steep slopes or cliffs and both are protected on the remaining side by the construction of double banks and ditches.

You should now retrace your steps to the marked footpath. As you walk back from the fort you may notice an outer bank under a field wall one and a half field lengths from the main earthworks. This was noticed and partially excavated in the 1990s. However, it is unclear if it is contemporary with the hillfort, in which case it could be an outer defended area or perhaps used for corralling animals; alternatively it could be a more recent field boundary, perhaps dating to medieval times.

Retrace your steps and take the path signposted to Ashford, this leads due south for a third of a mile before turning sharply to the left. After walking the length of one field, the way turns right again onto a track (Pennyunk Lane) which curves to the left towards Ashford. A quarter of a mile before the village, the path turns right across the fields, emerging near to the school. Walk through the village to the main road and turn right to the junction with the A6. Cross the road and turn right, walking towards Buxton for a third of a mile, then turn left into the lane signposted to Sheldon. After a few hundred metres, the road bends to the left and a footpath continues straight ahead. Follow this path alongside the river for almost a mile. The route then climbs up the slope, along the edge of Great Shacklow Wood. You should pass a 'crossroads' and a track joining from the left, after a further third of a mile another path joins from uphill and, after crossing a field boundary, you should bear right walking diagonally down the slope.

You should soon come to a signpost indicating Ashford, the way you have come, and Deepdale to the left. Another path leads straight ahead. In a while this will be your way on, first however, turn half left to explore a plateau area. This piece of land, known as Horsborough Plateau, once housed a Romano-British settlement. Pottery of this date has been found here and also some that may date to the Iron Age, it is possible that the area was occupied right through this period. In the north of this area, you can see the buried enclosure walls.

Return to the path and continue north-west along the east side of the plateau. After a hundred metres or so there is a stile with the path continuing ahead and a dark moss-covered ravine to the left. This is Demon's Dale and Late Neolithic or Early Bronze Age burials in the form of crouched inhumations have been found here. Continue on the easy path straight ahead and the car park is now just a few minutes walk.

Finding out more:

Preston, F 1954 'The hill-forts of the Peak' *DANHSJ* Vol 74

Wilson J & E English 1998 'Investigation of a ditch and bank at Fin Cop, Monsal Head, Ashford, Derbyshire' *DAJ*

Walk 13: Five Wells, Deepdale and Chee Tor

Distance: 11 miles (17.5km)

Starting Point: Taddington, SK143711. Park on the roadside in Taddington village.

Refreshments: There are pubs in Taddington and Chelmorton but take plenty of food and drink for the rest of the route.

Alternative Routes: You can visit Deepdale, Five Wells and Chelmorton in a 6 mile route described in Walk 13a or explore Chee Tor by walking from Miller's Dale (3½ miles) in Walk 13b.

Preamble

Five Wells chambered tomb is one of the more famous Peak District landmarks, located a few minutes walk from the Limestone Way, while Chee Tor is the best preserved of the many Romano-British settlements in terms of visible earthworks. This walk is quite long and is best undertaken on a warm summer's day with time to stop and picnic. The route is also a must for nature lovers; in May, Horseshoe Dale is full of orchids, while wild pansies flower on the hillside between Taddington and Five Wells. In the second half of the walk you have the option of braving the stepping stones on the River Wye or taking the drier route of the Monsal Trail. There is a steep climb up Chee Tor near the end of the route so remember to save some energy (or some chocolate!).

The Walk

Park your car in Taddington village. At the crossroads, take the turning posted Humphrey Gate and then turn immediately right onto the footpath to Chelmorton; this cuts diagonally across a field and then crosses Slipperlow Lane.

At the top of the hill, just before the reservoir, the barrow-like mounds are old mine workings. Closer inspection of the fields here also reveals wild pansies. Please note that this is private land and if you explore beyond the footpaths you do so at your own risk – beware of hidden mine entrances! Carry on past the reservoir and further covered shafts. The path crosses Sough Lane, part of the Limestone Way, and continues past Five Wells farm. Just after the farm, turn right into Pillwell Lane; after a few hundred metres there is a stile on the right and a concessionary path leads to Five Wells chambered tomb.

➡*Walkers following the longer route 13a rejoin here*

Five Wells chambered tomb dates to the Neolithic and archaeologists link it with Bole Hill (SK183677) as being one of a northern Derbyshire group of such monuments. Further south it is comparable with Minning Low and Green Low chambered tomb at Aldwark. It comprises two burial chambers constructed back to back and each accessed by a passage, hence the alternative term of passage grave. As you can see, the east-facing chamber is in slightly better condi-

The Five Wells chambered tomb

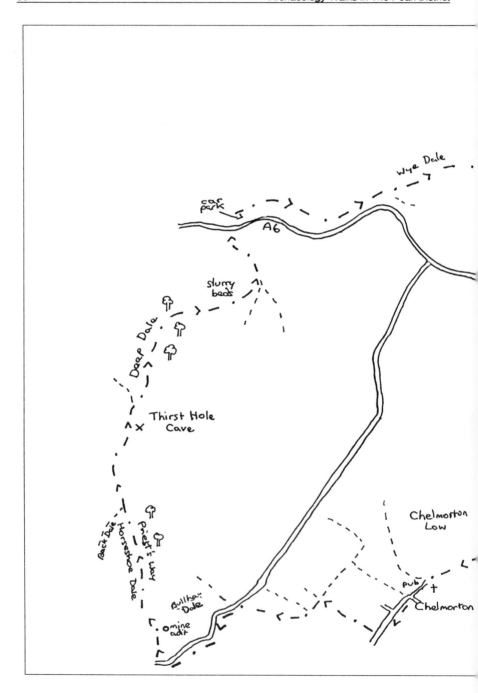

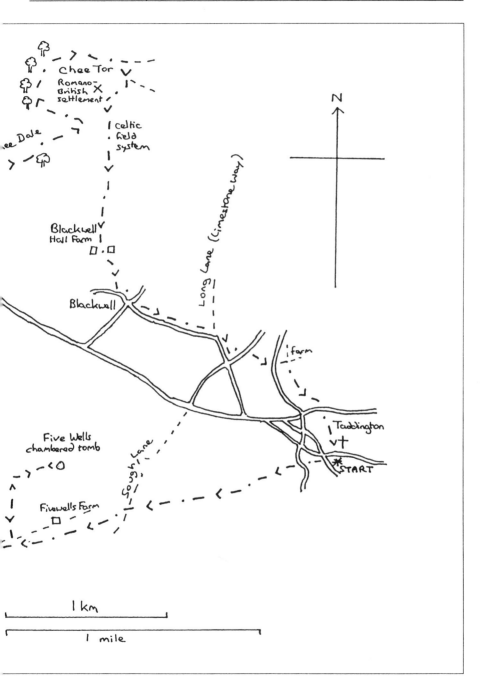

tion. The cap stones are now missing, as are some of the floor pavings, but portals and supporting side slabs are still in place.

The arrangement of leaning slabs appears rather sad and insignificant today but you are only seeing a fraction of the monument built 5000 years ago. The chambers were repositories for bones, each accommodating the remains of several individuals. It is also likely that the bodies were first defleshed, probably on raised platforms, then the clean bones were placed in the tomb. The monument was not a grave in terms of a final resting place but probably had great importance as a symbol of power, its position on a hilltop overlooking acres of land in several directions is no accident. We can only guess at the precise nature of the rites and ceremonies that went on here but it is very probable that bones were removed from the chambers and perhaps taken elsewhere or replaced with others. See also the descriptions for Minning Low and Long Low.

Archaeologists interpret the communal burial and deposition of bones in the Neolithic as representing an Ancestor cult. The treatment of the dead suggests that they were viewed as a whole, a unity of ancestors. It is likely that the presence of ancestral remains performed various functions such as establishing territory.

In the first stage of use, the slabs of the chambers and passages of Five Wells would have been covered by a cairn of stones. This must have looked very impressive gleaming white in the sunlight against the green of the hillside. Later the mound was enlarged and individual burials were placed within it – perhaps it had taken on the function of a Bronze Age barrow. During excavation, two crouched burials were found, one adjoining the perimeter wall and another within the cairn. Today you can still see the remains of the mound and the oval perimeter of the cairn, long since robbed of its stones, the chambers and passages have been partially back-filled to help preserve the monument.

Retrace your steps across the fields and back along Pillwell Lane, or, if you are following route 13a, turn left into the lane after leaving the concessionary path. Take the footpath to the right, opposite Five Wells Farm. This leads down into the village of Chelmorton.

➥ *Walkers on route 13a start here*

Chelmorton is the second highest village in England and retains most of its layout from medieval, possibly Anglo-Saxon, times when farmsteads lined the central street, each with long strips of land extending behind.

Take the footpath to the right half way down the street; after a few metres this crosses through the back garden of a cottage – don't worry, you are going the right way! After crossing some fields, turn left and take the second path on the right, this is a grassy lane bounded by walls. When you come to the road turn left and, immediately after the right-hand bend, go through the gate hidden behind trees on the right, into Horseshoe Dale. In May, the grassy slopes of this valley are sprinkled with orchids. You will soon come to a huge mine adit on the right, at the junction with Bullhay Dale. Continue straight ahead. You are now on the Priest's Way, the origin of this name is unclear but it is most likely that it is connected with the nearby Medieval grange – a farm owned by a monastery and worked by lay brethren. After three-quarters of a mile, the valley is joined by Back Dale and the two become Deep Dale.

After half a mile or so, look out for the caves on either side of the valley. A track leads up to a cave on your right, this extends back a good distance and the entrance is worth closer inspection. The cave is called Thirst Hole or sometimes Thirst House; the name is nothing to do with drinking but is a corruption of 'the hurst' meaning the hob hurst, the mythical capricious elf that crops up regularly in folklore. Excavations by Micah Salt at the end of the nineteenth century produced Roman or Romano-British finds both inside and outside the cave, they included such items as brooches and manicure and hairdressing items. Outside the entrance at the bottom of the slope were several burials, two were inhumations in an extended position while two were cremations. The cave has been interpreted as a domestic site but it seems strange to find comparatively high status objects in such a location and other Roman cave finds near Buxton have been referred to as caches. A recent review of the finds from Thirst Hole suggests that it was not a dwelling but the base for a Romano-British metal-working industry.

Keep to the right of the valley floor which gradually becomes marshy and forms a stream. Keep on the track passing to the east of the slurry beds and eventually returning to the valley floor.

➤ *Walkers on the shorter route 13a should turn right at the sign-posted path which leads them back into Chelmorton*

Cross the A6 (be careful – it's very busy) and turn right in the car park – this leads you to the path alongside the River Wye. After a short distance is the start of the Monsal Trail where a path follows the route of the old railway. You may either walk along this or stay on the path beside the river – there are regular connections between the two. If you stay on the riverside then be aware that short distances are slightly sporting with stepping stones, often quite widely spaced; however there is no real danger apart from that of getting your feet wet! After a very short distance you come to a bridge.

➤ *Walkers on route 13a to Five Wells, rejoin instructions for that walk*

Continue on this path for about 2 miles – it seems longer if you are walking beside the river. If you are on the Monsal Trail, rejoin the riverside path. Cross the river on the concrete footbridge signposted to Blackwell. Directly ahead is Chee Tor, a steep hill forming a promontory on a bend in the River Wye. Make your way up the hill, initially there are obvious paths but they soon disappear.

➤ *Walkers following route 13b join here*

At the top of the hill there are two stone walls built in a curved shape, one incomplete and the other forming the shape of a question mark. The Romano-British settlement occupies all of this area, you can see low banks covering the walls of many enclosures. These contained a variety of artefacts. Fragments of lead, lead ore and slag indicated that smelting was taking place while pieces of quern stone, bronze, glass, nails and boot studs suggested other activities. There was a considerable amount of pottery including sherds of samian ware, a fine Roman table ware coated in slip (a finely ground mixture of clay and water, often mistaken for a glaze). However, the most commonly occurring pottery was Derbyshire ware, a Roman coarse ware produced locally, possibly in Hazlewood near Belper.

Towards the west of the site, near to a present day field wall, a

Romano-British burial was excavated. It was found to be that of a female, between thirteen and nineteen years of age and small nodules of lead had been placed around her head. The burial is thought to date to the early to mid fifth century AD – in other words after the end of Roman rule.

The earthworks on Chee Tor are thought to represent a system of tracks, paths, buildings and enclosures – what we would probably regard as a village or hamlet. It is considered Romano-British, that is to say, it was occupied by native Britons under Roman occupation. For small farming communities, the Roman presence probably had little effect on everyday life. In the Peak District, a fringe area inbetween the Brigantes tribe to the north and the Coritani to the south, taxes and dues were probably paid to the local chiefs in much the same way as during the Iron Age. It is likely, though, that Roman lead mining in the Peak introduced new trading routes to the area with a wide variety of goods available for those who could afford them.

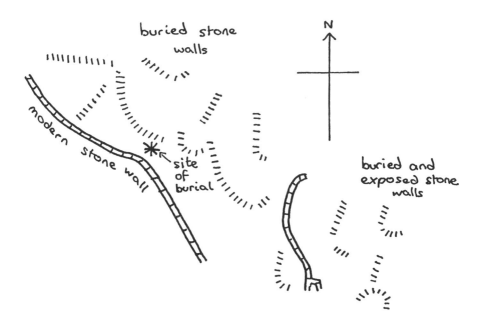

The Chee Tor Romano-British settlement

➡️*Walkers following route 13b should rejoin those instructions*

To the south of the main settlement, a footpath is marked over a stile in the stone wall. It leads past a pattern of Celtic or Anglo-Saxon field systems. Follow the path due south through Blackwell Hall farm and turn left onto the lane. Continue straight across at the crossroads (you should now be walking parallel to the A6) and after a quarter of a mile you briefly join the Limestone Way at Long Lane. The road bends to the right and you should almost immediately turn left to Priestcliffe. Take the footpath on the right after the second field boundary, when you emerge onto a road continue on the footpath on the opposite side. This brings you into Rock Lodge Farm and a footpath 'crossroads' where you should turn right. You should now be facing south-east on a path which leads across the fields to the A6 (take great care crossing) and resumes on the other side. Follow the path, which leads into Taddington via the churchyard, and pause to look at the cross (sadly not well preserved) before returning to your car.

Finding out more:

Branigan K & M Dearne 1991 'The small finds from Thirst House Cave, Deepdale: a reappraisal' in Hodges R & K Smith (eds) *Recent developments in the archaeology of the Peak*

Manby T G 1958 'Chambered tombs of Derbyshire' DANHSJ

Monet-Lane H C 1986 *The Romans in Derbyshire: Lead mining and the search for Lutudarum* (Veritas, Derbyshire)

Also, for Thirst Hole Cave, see reports by J Ward and M Salt in the DAJ 1895-1900

Walk 13a: Five Wells and Thirst Hole Cave

Distance: 8 miles (13km) or 4 miles (6km)

Starting Point: Chelmorton SK114702
Park near the church

Refreshments: There is a pub in Chelmorton.

Preamble

This walk is a shorter route to visit Thirst Hole Cave and Five Wells chambered tomb. It is particularly pleasant during May when orchids are in flower in Deepdale.

The Walk

➡️*Join Walk 13 where indicated.*

At the first bridge turn right onto the footpath. After a short distance, fork left over a stile and follow the path up the hillside. This path soon becomes a track, on reaching the driveway to Cottage Farm, turn right down to the A6. Continue along the track opposite, turning right where it finishes and then left through the gate marked 'Private land with public right of way'. After going through a further gate take the signposted path on the left to Fivewells cairn.

➡️*Rejoin Walk 13 where indicated.*

➡️*See map overleaf*

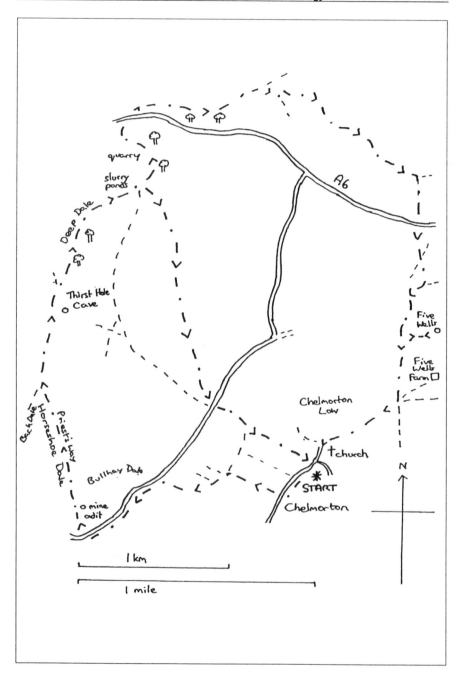

Walk 13b: Chee Tor and Miller's Dale

Distance: 3½ miles (5.5km)

Starting Point: Miller's Dale, SK138733. Park in the car park a few metres up the road to Wormhill.

Refreshments: Refreshments are available in Miller's Dale.

Preamble

This is a shortened route to visit the Romano-British settlement on Chee Tor. It is one of the best-preserved sites of its kind in the area with walls and enclosures clearly visible as earthworks. A footpath crosses the site but as a mark of courtesy please ask permission to explore the settlement at Blackwell Hall Farm. Although this is a short route, be prepared for some steep hills! The directions join Walk 13 for a full description of the earthworks.

The Walk

From Miller's Dale, cross the bridge and follow the road to Priestcliffe and Blackwell. After a few hundred metres take the track on the left, this is Long Lane, part of the Limestone Way. As you climb up the hill, look to your right (due west) and you may be able to make out some of the earthworks on Chee Tor. When you reach the road – you join it on a corner – turn right and continue straight ahead at the crossroads. After about a hundred metres, turn right to Blackwell Hall Farm. The route passes between the farm buildings, heading north up a track. After a right and left turn, the way becomes more of a path across the fields. Look out for Celtic field systems, you may be able to see the ancient field boundaries as low banks formed by ploughing.

Cross a stile onto Chee Tor. The right of way bears slightly to the right then the left, to arrive at the bottom of the steep slope at a footbridge. From the stile, the Romano-British settlement occupies the area immediately to the north and north-west.

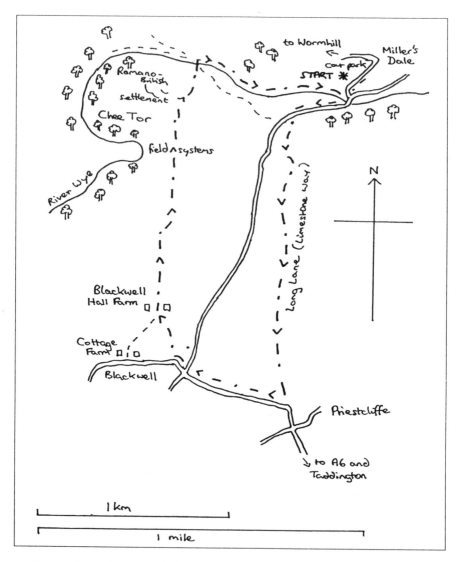

➡️*For a description of the settlement, join Walk 13 where indicated.*

Descend the hill and cross the bridge over the River Wye. Turn right
and either follow the riverside path or join the Monsal Trail back to
Miller's Dale.

Walk 14: Beeley Moor

Distance: 6 miles (10km)

Starting Point: SK265675. Park your car on the roadside in Beeley village.

Refreshments: There is a pub in Beeley.

Alternative Routes: Those wanting a longer walk may want to combine this with Walk 15 to Gardom's Edge. From Hob Hurst's House, a concessionary path leads north, round the boundary of the Chatsworth Estate and emerges onto the Chesterfield Road near the Robin Hood pub. From Gardom's Edge you can head north-west to Jack Flat, returning via Baslow, the Chatsworth Estate and Edensor for afternoon tea.

For a shorter route, drive up the road on the right of the pub and there is limited parking on the east corner of Hell Bank Plantation from where you can visit the moorland sites.

Preamble

This walk takes a scenic route through woodland, emerging onto Beeley Moor. The highlight of the trip is Hob Hurst's House, a burial monument of uncertain age but probably first built in the Bronze Age. Walkers should be aware that Beeley Moor is currently managed as a nature reserve and is accessed by concessionary paths. If you are carrying an Ordnance Survey map you may find that these differ from the marked public footpaths.

The Walk

Walk east along the road on the north side of the pub (the road to the south goes to Chesterfield). After a few hundred metres you will have left most of the houses behind and the way becomes narrow and winding. Beeley brook runs beside the road on the right.

At Moor Farm the main track bends to the farm buildings to the right while the footpath continues straight ahead up the hill. Soon after Moor farm is the wooded area of Beeley Plantation and Hell

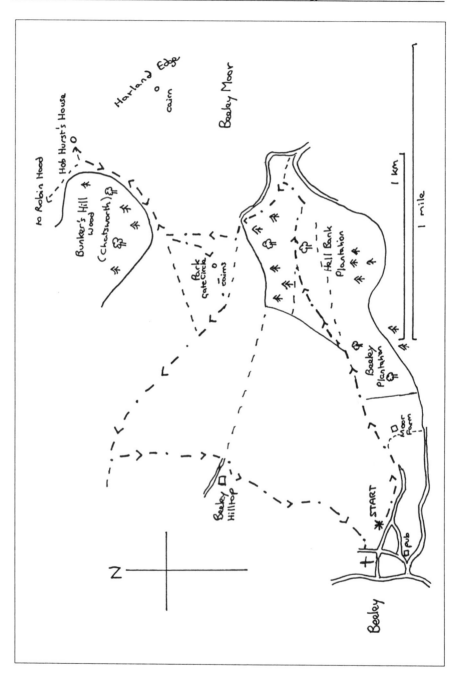

Bank Plantation. There are several gates leading into the wood, the first being probably the least steep of the paths. You can enter the wood at one of the lower gates or follow the path to the left of the wall and climb over the stile further up. The main paths lead you towards the north east corner of the wood, whereas you need to get to the most northerly point. You can either take the track to the left near the top of the hill or, if you find yourself on the road, turn left and follow the track round the perimeter of the wood.

You should now be at a junction of tracks and paths, on the edge of Beeley Moor. To the north is Bunkers Hill Wood; to the north west, Chatsworth House and to the north east, Harland Edge. Beeley Moor is a nature reserve accessed by concessionary paths which may not be marked on maps of the area.

Climb over the stile opposite. A well-trodden path leads to the west to Chatsworth and a few metres along a concessionary path turns off to the right and leads to Bunkers Hill Wood. Follow the concessionary path to the north. Near to the wall on the far side, the path turns to the right and crosses a stream. You then need to climb over a stile and walk up the slope, staying near to the boundary with the Chatsworth grounds. You should now have a good view of Harland Edge on your right. It is on nature reserve land so you can't explore but the area is important archaeologically. A cairn was excavated quite recently and photographs and artefacts are on display in Sheffield Museum. Meanwhile, in the woodland behind the wall on your left, a cave was excavated and a pot found dating to the Bronze Age. There was no evidence that it had been used as a burial site.

Continue up the slope until you reach the corner of the wall. From here, turn half right, along the path leading due east and after a few minutes you will come to Hob Hurst's House. The strange name is derived from a mythical elf said to haunt the woods (the name hob is used to refer to the devil) but in fact the cairn contained the remains of a very human individual. It is characterised by an unusually square bank and ditch surrounding the burial cist. The site was excavated in 1853 by Thomas Bateman but unfortunately archaeological methods used at the time have destroyed any dating evidence, archaeologists must rely on Bateman's written account of his

Part of the square ditch at Hob Hurst's House

fieldwork and on comparisons with similar sites to attempt to understand what happened here, and when.

Despite erosion and damage due to excavation, you can still see the central cairn surrounded by an unusually square ditch and bank; the bank originally had a circle of stones set into it. A primary cist – a box-like structure made of gritstone slabs – contained cremated bones. It was clear that the cremation happened in situ, in other words the cist was also the setting for the funeral pyre and the remains were placed in a corner with an arc of pebbles arranged around them. It has generally been accepted that the cairn and burial date to the Early Bronze Age although very few cairns or barrows of this date share the distinctive square structure. It could be that the monument was built in a different period in history or that it is a multi-phase site – perhaps a Bronze Age burial mound was modified and reused later in Anglo-Saxon times.

If you are continuing to Gardom's Edge you should turn to the north and follow the path alongside the perimeter of the Chatsworth Estate, otherwise you should retrace your steps down to the footpath 'crossroads'. At the point where you approached from the left, the

The cist in Hob Hurst's House (from Bateman 1861)

main path continues straight ahead, however, if you turn half left, a slightly less conspicuous track curves across the moor to a stone circle.

Park Gate is a small embanked circle with orthostats on the inner edge. It is difficult to be sure whether these are all intended as standing stones or whether some are part of a kerb.

Continue past the circle, you will pass the remains of several cairns and prehistoric fields and very soon join a well-trodden trackway. If you left your car on the roadside near the moor then turn left to return to your starting point, otherwise turn right onto this path and walk along the rather exposed section of moor. As you approach the civilisation of Chatsworth, follow the track round to the left. Soon a concessionary path is signposted to the left heading approximately due south. Follow this until you come to the farm at Beeley Hilltop. You will need to cross a stile, turning right onto the farm track, then turn almost immediately left over another stile onto a marked path. The route from here on is fairly obvious, skirting around the farm buildings before resuming its southerly direction, following the west side of a field boundary.

From here, you simply follow the stiles, crossing two fields diagonally before descending into Beeley via a grassy meadow and emerging onto the street almost opposite the church.

Finding out more:

Barnatt, J 1990 *The henges, stone circles and ringcairns of the Peak District* (University of Sheffield)

Bateman T 1861 *Ten years diggings in Celtic and Anglo-Saxon grave hills* (Smith, London)

Walk 15: Gardom's Edge

Distance: 3 miles (5km)

Starting Point: Birchen Edge car park, SK281721. Park your car in the public car park adjoining the Robin Hood pub.

Refreshments: The Robin Hood pub is next to the car park.

Preamble

Gardom's Edge is one of the richest areas of the Peak in terms of archaeology, and, during the 1990s, one of the most studied. At the time of writing, the last planned season of excavation is being organised. As such, features on the site will be described but detailed analyses of dating evidence or soil composition are not yet available; some of the comments on the Gardom's Edge features will therefore be speculative, to be confirmed or corrected in the future. This is a short walk but it includes a fairly steep hill climb. Those preferring longer walks may wish to combine it with Beeley Moor as described at the start of Walk 14.

The Walk

From the pub turn left onto the road and, after a few metres, cross the stile onto the moorland path. An information board confirms you are in the right place. Follow the path up the hill, passing a golf course and fields on your left. As the gradient levels out you can see the rockface of Birchen Edge on your right with the monument on top. At this point take the track that forks off to the left. Follow the path through the heather, it leads to an area of relatively flat ground with large clearings and clumps of trees.

Gardom's Edge is a shelf of moorland above Baslow and below Birchen Edge. It contains archaeological features from as far back as the Neolithic (4000-6000 years ago) up to the more recent post-medieval buildings and field boundaries. The terrain is covered by thickly growing heather hiding many of the features – much has been recognised comparatively recently – and birch woodland is currently regenerating. Stratigraphy has been important in understanding the archaeology; the peat is thought to have started forming in Roman times – therefore anything beneath it must have a prehistoric date. Areas excavated during the last few years have been cleared of trees and heather and left to regrow with turf so the archaeological features should be easier to see.

Make your way north-west towards the trees. In the central area two Late Bronze Age/Early Iron age houses have been excavated. You may be able to spot the one uncovered in 1998, it is a roughly circular stone structure abutting a natural stone outcrop. Fragments of pottery were found here together with half a shale bracelet.

A little to the north, in the trees, look for a linear feature of dips in the ground surface running east-west from Gardom's Edge towards Birchen Edge. This was originally thought to be some sort of boundary marker dating to Medieval or post-Medieval times. However, when one of the depressions was excavated in the summer of 1998, it turned out to be an alignment of pits. A bowl shape lined with clay was revealed; this was an exciting find because, although pit alignments are not uncommon, the clay lining, causing the feature to retain water, is exceptional. It is likely that these features functioned

Excavation of one of the clay-lined pits

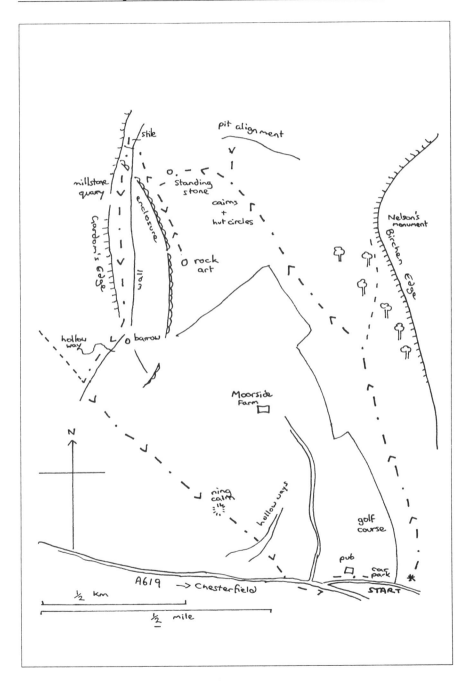

as a boundary but we do not know whether they had a practical use or a more spiritual purpose. However, the stratigraphy makes it likely that they date to the Bronze or the Iron Age.

Between the standing stone and the Edge is a huge semi-circular bank, constructed with large boulders and thought to date to the Neolithic. Again it is unclear whether it formed a practical or a spiritual boundary but it is very possible that it is a Peak District equivalent of the concentric circles of pits and ditches known as causewayed enclosures in the south of England. It is thought that such places may have fulfilled several functions including feasting, the culling of livestock and exposure of the dead to be defleshed. We have no way of knowing if the enclosure at Gardom's Edge was used for this purpose because the soil is so acidic that no traces of bone could survive.

To the east of the enclosure bank and south of the standing stone is a boulder decorated with rock art; or – to be more precise – there is a fibre-glass cast. The original was eroding so quickly due to pollution that it has been reburied in an effort to preserve what is left. The carving would have been made by pecking – hitting the surface with

Prehistoric rock art

a hard stone and similar examples of such art have been found elsewhere in the Peak District. The most common components of these designs are circular depressions and spirals known as cup and rings. Similar decorated stones, thought to date to the Neolithic, are found in other parts of Britain; they are especially prolific in Scotland – probably because of better preservation.

Follow the Neolithic enclosure to the north, eventually it continues on the other side of a field wall. A few metres north of this point, a stile leads to the left. Be careful to restrain children and dogs – a few feet away is the precipitous drop over the edge. Turn left again, heading south along the edge. Down the slope to the right are the old trackways of an abandoned millstone smithy together with some domed millstones in situ.

Continue south close to the wall. You will cross more of the Neolithic bank and pass a Bronze Age barrow and a hollow way leading from an old gate in the wall. Continue down the slope until a path joins from the right. Follow this path to the left across a field. You should pass a ringcairn and further hollow ways. The path heads east and emerges onto the Chesterfield road a few hundred metres west of your starting point.

Finding out more:

Ainsworth S & J Barnatt 1998 A scarp edge enclosure at Gardom's Edge, Baslow, Derbyshire. *DAJ*

Barnatt J & P Reeder 1982 'Prehistoric rock art in the Peak District' *DAJ*

Hart C 1985 'Gardom's Edge, Derbyshire: Settlements, cairnfield & hillfort' in Spratt D & C Burgess (eds) *Upland settlement in Britain* (Oxford BAR 143)

Radley J 1964 'A millstone maker's smithy on Gardom's Edge, Baslow' *DAJ*

www.shef.ac.uk/~geap/ 'Archaeological Investigations of a Peakland Landscape'

Walk 16: The Edges – Baslow, Curbar and Froggatt

Distance: 11 miles (18km).

Starting Point: Baslow SK255722. Baslow is located at the junction of the A623 and the A619. Park either in the village or, alternatively there is a car park to the south-east of the village, just south of the A619.

Refreshments: Hot food and drinks are available at Grindleford Cafe half way round the walk and there is a cafe at Calver Bridge.

Preamble

This walk combines striking views from the edges with a gentle riverside stroll on the return. It visits a Bronze Age cremation cemetery at Eaglestone Flat, the Stoke Flat stone circle on Froggatt Edge and the ruined medieval manor at Padley Chapel. Although it is quite a long route, more than half the way is on level ground. The walk is based from Baslow where there is parking, refreshments and an Anglo-Saxon cross in the porch of the church.

The Walk

Leave Baslow along Bar Road. This starts as a well-maintained lane heading north-east from the village. The road turns a double bend and climbs quite steeply up the hill with plantations on the right. As you near the top of the edge there is a gate and information board.

On top of Baslow Edge the path divides; the right hand fork leading to the east, past Wellington's monument, and the left leading north along the top of the edges. Your route lies along the path to the left. The triangle of land enclosed within the fork is called Eaglestone Flat and you can see the Eagle Stone, reputedly an object of worship for Celtic people, near to the path. Remains on this patch of land date to the Bronze Age and encompass a time period spanning several hundred years. Excavation revealed field systems with

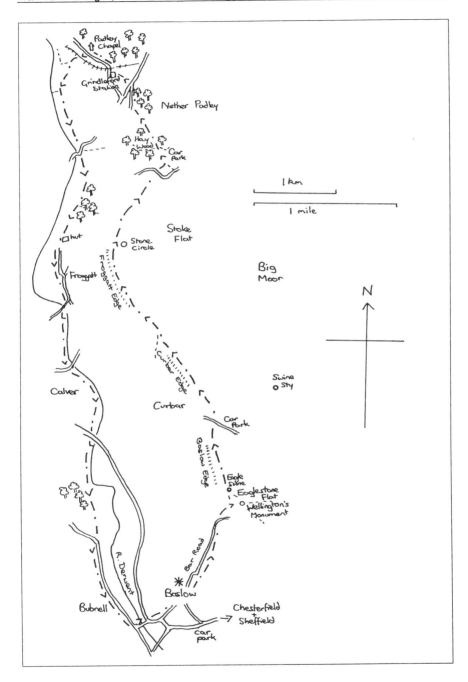

an area of cultivated land bounded by low stone walls. At some point, the walled area became a cremation cemetery housing at least fifteen bodies, placed either in urns or directly into the ground. There was also evidence of funeral pyres. Grave goods included stone tools, a bone flute (buried with a child) and faience beads. Although the Eagle Stone itself is a natural feature, it is almost certain that importance was attached to it, hence the nearby burials.

Cross the road and walk through the gate and up Curbar Edge to your left. As you climb onto higher ground you will gain commanding views to your left. Meanwhile, to the east, the rather bleak aspect of Big Moor stretches into the distance. Although it does not look very welcoming today, in prehistoric times this area was well used. Although they cannot be seen during this walk, some of the features there are worth mentioning. To the east, the Bar Brook stone circles are quite spectacular and on the south end of the moor, Swine Sty is a circular structure dating to the late Bronze Age. Interpreted as a stone-footed building, it is likely that it was built largely of timber stone base or foundations and excavations suggest that it was used to manufacture shale items such a bracelets. Nearby are the remains of prehistoric field systems as well as cairnfields – sometimes representing burials and others clearance mounds enabling the land to be cultivated and monuments to be built. Big Moor is managed as a sanctuary area and anyone wanting to visit it should contact the Peak Park office in Bakewell.

On Froggatt Edge, in an area with a sprinkling of trees, Stoke Flat stone circle lies just a few metres to the right of the path. The monument stands out because of a tall standing stone marking the southern entrance. The circle comprises a rubble bank with drystone walling on the inside and the remains of two rings of standing stones. Although only a few are left today, Thomas Bateman recorded the site in the mid 19th century and noted that the stones were evenly spaced. Some reports state that the Duke of Rutland excavated a cremation burial with an urn in this area in the early part of the twentieth century. However, it is unclear whether this information is accurate and, if it is, whether the finds were within the circle or from a nearby cairn. Sadly, it seems that much of the site has been destroyed during the last 150 years. Various alignments have been noted for the position of the circle. Perhaps the most interesting is that, when viewed from Stoke Flat, the full moon at midsummer sets directly over Arbor Low henge on the distant horizon.

Continue along the path. A prehistoric field system has also been identified in the area to your right. It is clear that these gritstone uplands were much less bleak and exposed two or three thousand years ago and that they were well used by our ancestors both for ritual and domestic/agricultural purposes.

The path continues along the edge then eventually descends, bending to the right before emerging onto the road. Turn right onto the road and your way continues on the footpath to the left just a few metres ahead.

You now cut across a small field and turn left (now heading due north), leaving a car park on your right. After walking through Hay Wood for about a quarter of a mile, keep going straight ahead on the same contour, ignoring the more obvious path that goes downhill to your left. After a further half mile you join a narrow lane, turn right and this leads you down to the main road through Nether Padley. Just a few metres ahead, a footpath on the left is signposted to Grindleford Station.

Grindleford Cafe (the old station building) is a good place to stop for a mug of tea and a chip buttie. When you have rested and eaten enough, walk north from the station, over the bridge and along the track that bends to the left alongside the railway.

It is less than half a mile to Padley Chapel, the only surviving remnant of Padley Hall, a fourteenth century manor. If you go behind the chapel you can see the remains of rooms and a spiral staircase. A further range once extended across to the railway line on the other side of the track.

Return to the track and take the footpath on the left immediately after the field centre. This leads over the railway and then follows the field boundary towards the river. Halfway down fork left and cross the adjacent field in a south-westerly direction, when you come almost to the river, turn half left through a gate and follow the path until you come to the road. Cross the road then take the footpath adjacent to the bridge, this crosses a field diagonally. Climb over the stile into the field beyond and follow the path as it goes

Remains of the manor at Padley Chapel

south into Horse Hay Coppice. The way continues a short distance within the trees for about half a mile before emerging again onto fields. The river is always one or two fields away on your right. Soon after leaving the woods, the path seems to disappear and there is an old stone building straight ahead. Keep to the right of the wall and you will find yourself in a narrow track (Spooner Lane), this brings you into Froggatt village.

When you come to a road, bear right and you will soon come to a bridge. Cross the bridge, then turn immediately left onto the river-side path. After half a mile you will need to fork left onto the Froggatt Road, cross the road, then rejoin the river path, veering temporarily away from the waterside at Stocking Farm. When you come out onto the road, Calver Mill is signposted. Refreshments are available at shops and cafes near here.

The footpath continues along the west bank of the river, passing under the road (A623). Soon the river bends sharply to the left but you should carry on straight ahead, along the edge of St Mary's wood. The trees give way to some open marshy ground and a stile accesses a short cut to the lane into Bubnell. Turn left into this road and it is now a little less than a mile until a bridge on the left leads to the main street of Baslow.

Finding out more:

Barnatt J 1978 *Stone Circles of the Peak* Turnstone books, London.

Barnatt J 1994 Excavations of a Bronze Age unenclosed cemetery, cairns and field boundaries at Eaglestone Flat, Curbar, Derbyshire. *Proceedings of the Prehistoric Society* 60

Walk 17: Cairns and Circles on Eyam Moor

Distance: 10 miles (16km) or 7 miles (11km)

Starting Point: Sir William Hill Road, about 1½ miles north of Eyam, SK224780. Eyam is best approached by a short lane from the A623. You should then follow the road to the left, past the car park, then bending right as it winds out of the village. Park near the junction of Sir William Hill Road and Edge Road. Most people turn left and park at the start of this track.

Refreshments: There are pubs and cafes in Eyam.

Preamble

Eyam Moor was a popular place in the Bronze Age. Stone circles, cairns and ringcairns are hidden amongst the grass and heather, there is even an example of rock art from that time. The most impressive monuments are Wet Withens, a stone circle located right in the centre of the moorland, and an adjacent cairn. This walk is suitable for anyone who enjoys orienteering, the area is only about four square miles so there's no danger of getting seriously lost! The walk is planned from the edge of the moor so you have the option of returning directly to the car (the short route) or continuing into Eyam to benefit from the facilities, visit the cross and explore the history of the 'plague village'. You may of course walk the shorter route then drive into Eyam for refreshments. Regular grid references are given on this walk to help identify features of interest.

The Walk

On the opposite side of this junction are two footpaths and you should take the one that forks to the right. Follow this path (roughly north-east) for almost a mile, stopping about two hundred metres before the field boundary.

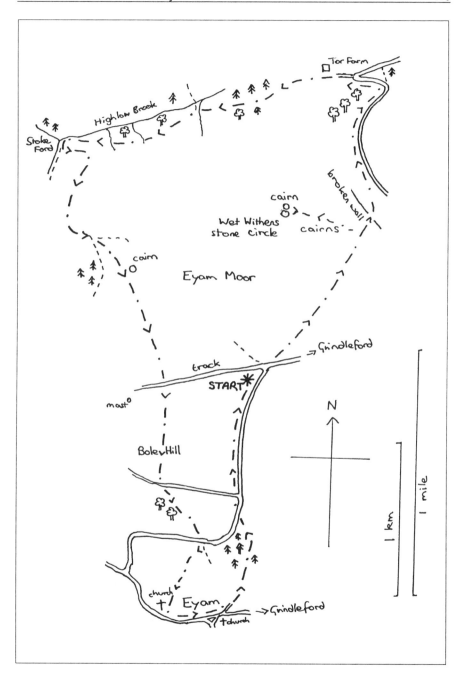

At this point you need to leave the path, the usual rules apply – try not to cause any damage or disturb ground-nesting birds.

The first two features are an optional extra – you may enjoy the challenge of trying to locate them. One is right beside the path but even so, it can be very difficult to spot low stones in the heather; on my recent visit to the moor, in rain and mist, I failed to find either of them!

The first circle is close to the path at SK23227879. Listed in archaeology reports as Eyam Moor III, it is a free-standing stone circle, that is, there is no surrounding rubble bank; this is unusual for Peak District circles. When Thomas Bateman first discovered this monument, a hundred and fifty years ago, it comprised nine stones (although three had fallen) and had a central mound. Now there are only six stones, four of them still standing, and the central cairn has obviously suffered as a result of excavation.

The next circle is located at SK23157895 so you need to walk north-west for about a hundred metres. Known as Eyam Moor II, this is an embanked stone circle and, of the seven described by Bateman, four small stones now line the inner edge. If the stones were evenly spaced then there would originally have been nine.

The next two features are much more distinctive. Stop about two hundred metres before the broken wall and then turn due west, walking in this direction for about half a mile. You will pass the remains of several cairns, look out for kerb stones and rocks forming the small enclosed areas of central cists. After about ten minutes, you should see a large cairn. Despite extensive damage, it is still very distinctive and is further identified by an information board. Immediately south of the cairn is Wet Withens stone circle (SK225790), it is on a north facing shelf not far from the steep drop into Bretton Clough. Wet Withens is a large circle of more than 30 yards (27 metres) in diameter, it is enclosed by a continuous bank – the apparent dips are the result of erosion from more recent paths. First reports of this site date to the eighteenth century when it was said to have sixteen standing stones. By the time of Bateman's visit in the mid nineteenth century there were thirteen and you may observe that the number is further reduced today. Like many Peak District circles, a large number of the stones are leaning or fallen but this may be due more to a design fault in the construction rather than deliberate or accidental damage. Having said that, we must assume that the missing stones did not remove themselves!

Some accounts from the nineteenth century report that Wet Withens once had a central cairn – even a burial. Like other areas within the Peak, the problem with reports of this date is in establishing the exact location to which they refer. Without modern surveying techniques and positioning systems, they rely largely on visual details which can be ambiguous, particularly on open moorland. There is no apparent trace of excavation within Wet Withens circle so for the time being we must assume that these reports refer to another feature close by – perhaps the large, badly damaged cairn to the north.

Retrace your steps to the east until you rejoin the path. If you come to a wall then turn right and follow it and you will come to the footpath. The way now turns to the left and descends the slope to join the road at Leam. Turn left onto the road and follow it for half a mile. There is a sharp right-hand bend and, shortly after, one to the left, your way ahead is down the track to the left towards Tor Farm, part way round this second bend.

The path continues due west through a gate, leaving the farm buildings on the right. Shortly after, it bends to the left, adjacent to the field boundary. After a quarter of a mile, the path bends to the right through Highlow Wood, it then turns left uphill. It is about a mile now to Stoke Ford, the confluence of Highlow and Bretton Brooks – don't be confused by the smaller streams that join from the hillside on the left.

At Stoke Ford, turn left and follow the path alongside Bretton Brook, after a short distance, take the steep path to the left. Follow this route as it winds its way up the slope until, after about two thirds of a mile the path crosses a stile and branches into three. Ways to the left and right follow the field boundaries but you should take the middle path directly up the hill.

If you are following the Ordnance Survey map, the site you are now seeking – or hopefully have found – is marked as a ringcairn, a circular bank of stones or rubble. It is adjacent to the path, on your left, roughly in line with the corner of Gotherage Plantation. In fact, archaeologists have recently re-evaluated the feature at SK21547865 and now think that it was originally a cairn, a huge mound of stones, but that the material from the interior has been robbed. These handy building blocks, probably now featuring in nearby stone walls, have left an obvious space in the centre leading to the misinterpretation but evidence of disturbance suggests that this was the most likely course of events. There is, however, a stone in the central area that has been carved with shallow depressions called cupmarks. This would date to the Neolithic or Bronze Age and was achieved by pecking – hitting the stone with a hard rock or pebble to crush the surface.

A 'cup-marked' stone in a robbed cairn

Continue along the path in a south-south-easterly direction until you come to Sir William Hill Road. You now have the choice of turning left along this track to return directly to your car. Alternatively, to visit Eyam and complete the longer circuit, cross the road and take the path opposite. This route will add three or four miles and a steep hill to your walk!

Follow the path which leads south over Bole Hill. This name usually denotes an area once used for smelting ore – especially that of lead. It is reputed, although not proven, that the hill was used for this purpose in Roman times.

When you come to the road, the path is almost opposite – a little to the left – and leads in a south-easterly direction, soon descending steeply down Eyam Edge. On reaching the next road you can either turn right onto it or take either of the paths opposite, all these routes will bring you down into Eyam. However, I recommend taking the middle route – the path that leads directly downhill. At the bottom of the hill, a gate leads into the churchyard. At the front of the church, stop to look at the cross. This finely preserved piece of An-glo-Saxon masonry dates to the eighth century. You may also notice that the name on the headstone nearby is Froggatt – illustrating how common it was to take your name from your home town or village. Presumably, this person or their ancestors had moved a few miles down the road.

Leave the village on the Grindleford road and take the fork to the left (Riley Back) opposite a chapel. Turn immediately right and at the end of the road, fork up the hill to the left along the path that climbs, due north, through woodland. Curving around the edge of the trees, it meets Hollow Brook before joining the back road to Grindleford. Turn right onto Edge Road and follow it north for about half a mile until the junction with Sir William Hill Road.

Finding out more:

Barnatt, J 1990 *The henges, stone circles and ringcairns of the Peak District* (University of Sheffield)

Walk 18: Carl Wark, Upper Padley and Hathersage

Distance: 8 miles (13km).

Starting Point: Hathersage, SK232814. Park in Hathersage, there is a car park in Oddfellows Road behind the main street.

Refreshments: There are refreshments available at Grindleford Station Cafe and in Hathersage.

Alternative Routes: This walk can be split into two halves by catching the train between Hathersage and Grindleford.

Preamble

This walk begins with a scenic stroll along the river to Nether Padley, pausing on the way to look at the ruins of the manor at Padley Chapel. After a refreshment break at Grindleford Cafe, the way continues through Padley Gorge to Lawrence Field. The route climbs up to the ancient fort of Carl Wark, then drops into Hathersage via Higger Tor and Camp Green, an earthwork dating to Norman times. This walk is pleasant all year round although the moorland around Carl Wark can become rather waterlogged after rainy weather. Grindleford is served by trains on the Sheffield to Manchester line and you may wish to vary the walk by catching the train from Hathersage to Grindleford, but check the timetable first as the service may be infrequent especially on Sundays.

The Walk

Leave Hathersage on the Grindleford/Abney road, passing the turning to the station on your left. The River Derwent crosses under the road after a quarter of a mile and you should turn left onto the footpath immediately before, leading to the north-east bank of the river. Follow the riverside path for about a mile then take the track that bears left uphill, towards the wall and trees. You will soon be sign-

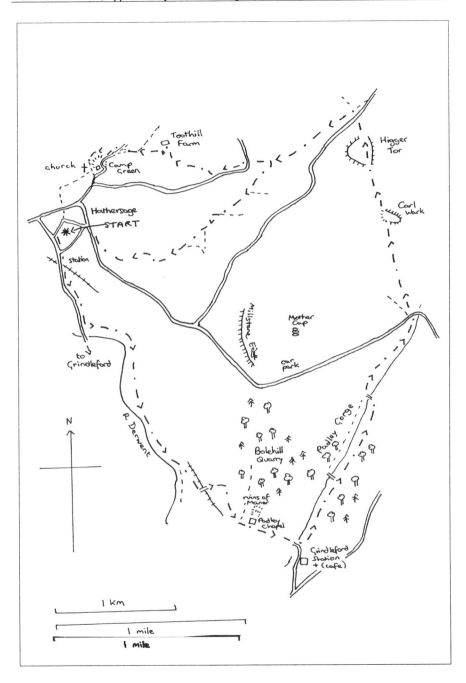

Toothill Farm

Higger Tor

church

Camp Green

Carl Wark

Hathersage
START

station

to Grindleford

Millstone Edge

Mother Cap

car park

Padley Gorge

N

R. Derwent

Bolehill Quarry

ruins of Manor

Padley Chapel

Grindleford Station + (cafe)

1 km

1 mile

1 mile

posted left and cross the railway via a bridge. A few hundred metres north of the railway, turn right onto the well-defined path. Stay on this path until you come to Padley Chapel on your left, there is a field centre opposite on the right.

The chapel is the only surviving range of a fourteenth century manor. Part of the building was lost under the railway and field centre but if you look behind the chapel you can see the remains of walls and a spiral staircase.

You may now want to make a short detour to look at Bolehill Quarry. This can be reached by retracing your steps a few metres and taking the path leading uphill into the trees immediately before Padley Chapel. The quarry occupies an extensive area, stretching north to the main road.

Abandoned grindstones in Bolehill Quarry

The rock in this area is known as gritstone or millstone grit. As its name suggests, it has an industrial history, somewhat chequered by the fashions of the day. Quern stones, dating as far back as the Neolithic and Bronze Age have been found on Beeley Moor. The use of this rock for grinding corn continued through prehistory and history, with the dressed stones changing from saddle shaped to the more familiar circular shape by Medieval times. Then, in the mid nineteenth century, it became fashionable to eat white bread rather than wholemeal and the coarse stone was not suitable for milling fine white flour. After a short break, new uses were found for the stone, for building material and, during the early stages of its development, as a grindstone for Sheffield steel.

The prime use of the quarry at Bole Hill was in providing building stone for the reservoir dams north of Bamford. This was extracted in the first few years of the twentieth century. Before and since, grindstones were produced and many can still be seen abandoned at the bottom of the slopes, marking the time when they too were superseded by modern technology.

Return to Padley Chapel and continue along the path to Grindleford Station. After an optional stop for refreshments (the station cafe is famous for its chip butties!) walk back along the road, over the railway line, then turn right, through the gate, into Padley Gorge. The path is labelled Longshaw Estate and runs close to the east bank of the river. You can either follow this route through the gorge, or for added interest, it is possible to cross the river at various places, via footbridges and stepping stones, or even, in hot weather, by a more direct route! The woods in this area are thought to be typical of the mixed deciduous woodland that grew during the Neolithic – about 5000 years ago – with birch, oak, elm and hazel. Hornbeam and lime also grew in central and southern England and alder and willow flourished beside rivers and marshes.

After a mile and a half, the path emerges onto the open land of Lawrence Field. You will need to cross to the west of the river if you have not done so already, there is a footbridge soon after the margin of the trees. The way ahead lies along this riverside path towards Carl Wark, the lower and nearer of the two hills directly ahead. However, you may first wish to spend some time exploring the archaeology of Lawrence Field. On the site of this medieval farm, you may be able to spot field systems and earthworks of two buildings in the eastern corner. In order to prepare the land for arable cultivation, narrow strips were cleared of stones and boulders, the waste material being piled into cairns.

Return to the path beside the river and continue north until you reach the road, a sharp bend should be just to your right. From here, any of the paths opposite will lead up to Carl Wark. The most established track is a few hundred metres down the road to the right, but be warned, if you go this way you will have to cross a stream requiring a bold step! A second path begins at the bend in the road but this can sometimes be waterlogged. The most accessible route is probably across the stile directly opposite where the way ahead is on slightly higher ground.

You should now head directly up to the south-west corner of Carl Wark; you will, however, have to cross a short stretch of boggy ground first. This is best negotiated by veering slightly to the right.

Until the last decade or so, it was thought that the defended enclosure of Carl Wark was built in Anglo-Saxon times, around AD500-800. The main argument for this was its construction; the use of a turf rampart with revetting stones bonded into it was similar to Scottish structures of this date. However, the inward-bending entrance is indicative of the Iron Age and other settlements of this period are known to have existed nearby. It is now generally thought that the first defences were built in the Iron Age (around 500BC), and that further fortifications may have been added in Roman times. At the same time, it is very possible that, like Mam Tor, the hilltop was occupied before this. Take some time to explore the area, you will notice that the stone wall is only built around the south-west where the slope of the land is more gentle. An information board just around the corner from the entrance gives further details. There is an abandoned millstone lying in situ near the base of the north-east corner of the hill.

When you have finished exploring Carl Wark, continue from the wall on the west along the path to Higger Tor, the slightly higher hill to the north-west. As you climb, turn back and appreciate the aerial view of Carl Wark. It requires a few scrambling manoeuvres to gain the summit of Higger Tor. There appear to be no archaeological references to this peak, yet at the same time it would appear an equally, if not superior, candidate for a hillfort as Carl Wark. As always in ar-

The southern wall on Carl Wark

chaeology, lack of evidence does not mean an area was not used in the past and, in this case, we should, perhaps, stay open-minded.

Continue to the far side of the hilltop. To the left, you can see Hathersage and straight ahead you can see the road and your path. Descend the steps, cross the road and take the path opposite. After a few minutes, turn left onto the well-trodden path; this soon joins a farm track. You now have a choice of two routes into Hathersage. The most well-used way turns left off the gravel track onto a sign-posted footpath. Stay on this route and it leads into the village. Alternatively, continue along the track a few metres further and you come to a road. Turn left onto the road then right onto the farm track after a few hundred metres. This leads to Toothill Farm where you need to turn left. The right of way goes through two sets of gates (please be careful to shut them) into the farmyard, turning left in front of the farm buildings. A track then winds back to the left for a few metres where there is a squeeze stile into the field to the right. Cross to the far side of this field then turn left, following the hedge on the north-east side. Look out for the stile in the corner which joins what appears to be an old hollow way. After a few metres this comes out onto a more substantial, tarmacked drive.

It is now only a few metres to Camp Green. This feature, thought to be an early Norman ringwork is just to the north-east of the church, located on a knoll of shale outcrop. The structure comprises a circular earthwork defended by a ditch and a revetted rampart five metres wide and over a metre high. If you stay on the track you will cross part of the ditch but you will probably see more by going through the iron gate on your right and following the path round. Approximately one third of the bank and ditch can be seen in the garden to your left just before you come to the church. It is unclear what this feature was for as there is no substantial mound (motte) on which to build a keep. The current theory is that such structures date to early Norman times and may have had some administrative purpose such as controlling hill farmers. However, there is no clear dating evidence and the possibility remains that Camp Green and similar earthworks are attributable to the early Britons or the Danes.

Before you return to your car via the tea shops, you may want to look round the front of the church. Here you can see the much eroded base of a pre-Norman cross and – reputedly, but not archaeo-logically substantiated – the grave of Little John of Robin Hood fame.

Finding out more:

Hodges R 1980 'Excavations at Camp Green, Hathersage (1976-7) a Norman ringwork' *DAJ*

Preston, F 1954 'The hill-forts of the Peak' *DANHSJ* Vol 74

Walk 19: Mam Tor and Navio

Distance: 11 miles (19km).

Starting Point: Odin Mine, SK135834. Park your car on the road near to Odin's Mine. This is reached by going west out of Castleton and continuing along the road past Treak Cliff Cavern rather than forking left into Winnat's pass.

Refreshments: There are pubs and cafes in Castleton and Hope. At the time of writing there were also refreshments available at Lose Hill Farm.

Alternative Routes: Walk 19a visits Mam Tor and Castleton, Walk 19b visits Castleton and Navio.

Preamble

This walk spans several periods in history and prehistory. The higher ground was occupied during the Bronze Age and Iron Age, the most well known and spectacular part being the hillfort of Mam Tor. On the lower ground near Hope, is the site of the Roman fort of Navio. The small town of Castleton is at the heart of the walk and you may wish to spend some time here, visiting Peveril Castle or one of the mines open to the public as show caves. The section from Odin Mine to Lose Hill is quite strenuous but you are rewarded with breathtaking views on a clear day.

The Walk

The first feature on this walk is Odin Mine. On the left of the road you can see the cleft in the hillside where the vertical seam of lead ore has been extracted, while on the right are the wheel and track of the ore crushing circle. According to local tradition, Odin Mine was worked from Roman times and although this may be true there is no evidence to support it; it was, however, in use from at least the thirteenth century. The name is said to derive from its being worked at the time of the Danes.

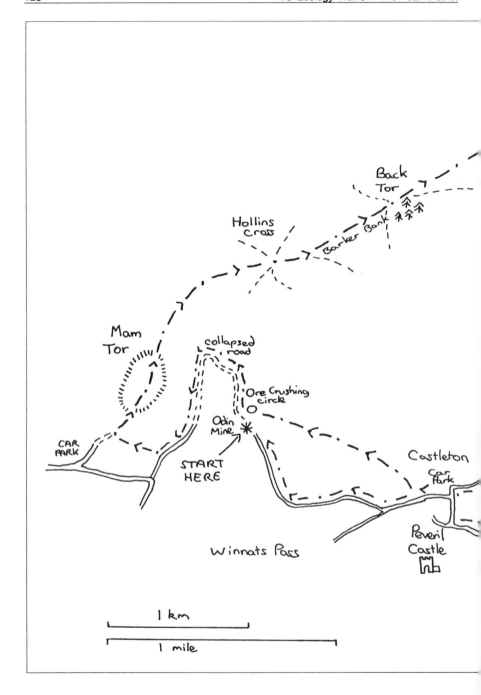

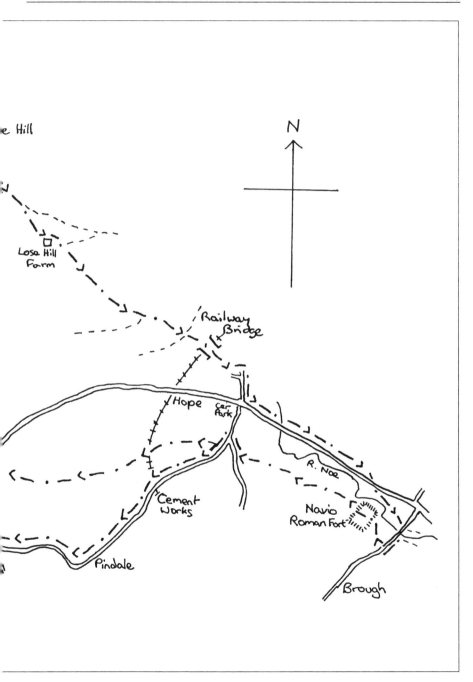

The ore crushing circle at Odin mine

Continue along the road, which soon turns sharply to the left, climbing up towards Mam Tor. This was originally part of the main trunk road from Manchester to Sheffield but landslips forced it to be abandoned. The problem is caused by the geology of the area, where beds of shale are sliding downhill. If you look up at Mam Tor, you will see more evidence of this where similar land movement has literally taken a slice out of the hillside. This phenomenon has earned it the name of the Shivering Mountain.

Continue along the disused road and through the gate at the end. Signposts to Mam Tor direct you along the road. After a quarter of a mile, a concessionary path across National Trust land to the right is clearly marked to Mam Tor. Follow this path until you turn right to join the main route leading up Mam Tor. The climb up the hill is helped by a well-maintained path with stone steps. Near the top you can see part of the defensive ditch on your right, believed to have been dug during the Iron Age. At its maximum, the height of the bank from the bottom of the ditch is thirty feet! On top of the hill, a new path was built by archaeologists in the mid 1990s (the paving slabs were lifted onto the hilltop by helicopter). This was a rescue

Mam Tor

project because the original track was so well-used that the ramparts that had stood for over 2000 years were rapidly being eroded. Archaeologists believe that the ramparts we see today – the huge earthen bank with external ditch – were preceded by a ditch and timber palisade.

Mam Tor is the best known of the Peak District hillforts and, at sixteen acres (6.4 hectares), the largest – although it is considered small when compared with those in other parts of the country such as Maiden Castle in Dorset or Uffington Castle near Wantage. Although the hilltop comprises very uneven ground, unusual for a hillfort, excavations have revealed the remains of Bronze Age houses built on terraced platforms. It seems that the area was inhabited from about 1700 – 1000BC (dates suggested from radiocarbon analysis of the house platforms) and that the defensive structures were added up to a thousand years later. Also within the enclosure are two Bronze Age barrows which could have been built before the hilltop became a dwelling site. As with many archaeological sites spanning a long period of time, we cannot be sure whether Mam Tor was inhabited continuously or sporadically.

Follow the path across the top of Mam Tor and as you leave the fort on the north side you can see more of the great ditch. After half a mile, you come to Hollins Cross where several paths join. The remains of a bole was found near here. This is a hearth where ores were smelted and many were located throughout the Peak District, accounting for the common use of the name 'Bole' or 'Bole Hill'.

➡ *Walkers following route 19a should now turn to the instructions for that walk*

Continue along the path straight ahead, climbing up Back Tor. This is a distinctive hill with coniferous woods on the east side and steep rocky cliffs with spectacular views over the Vale of Edale to the west. It is a good place to stop for a break on a warm calm day. During the 1980s, natural erosion of the shale grit on this hilltop exposed various artefacts. These included a fragment of a shale bracelet similar to those found on Mam Tor, a bronze socketed knife and a thick walled pot, all dating to the Late Bronze Age or Early Iron Age. Meanwhile, scatters of flint blades could have been produced as early as the Neolithic. Based on these finds, archaeologists have suggested that Back Tor may have been a domestic site or a burial ground – possibly with a barrow built on the highest point. Pieces of lead ore (galena) suggest that there was a bole nearby.

A further half mile brings you to the top of Lose Hill where directions are indicated to surrounding places. You should follow the pointer for Hope and take the path to the south-east. After a quarter of a mile, cross the stile on your right but continue in the same direction following the field boundary.

After a further quarter of a mile, you should come to Lose Hill Farm. At the time of writing, the farm was open as a nature trail and for refreshments. Follow the track to the left, to the north of the farm buildings then take the path marked to the right, immediately after the livestock enclosures. This route continues to the south-east, sometimes along field boundaries and sometimes within a walled or hedged lane. Beware! This area can be very damp underfoot. A rather interesting modern bridge crosses the railway and the path continues into Hope, emerging alongside the school.

➡️ ***Walkers following route 19b join here***

Hope has considerable history, having once housed an Anglo-Saxon manor; today it is a good place to stop for lunch if you have not brought your own refreshments. Afterwards walk east along the main road. About half a mile out of the village, you can see a roadsign ahead pointing right to Brough. You can either continue along the road to this junction or cross the road and take the footpath diagonally across the field. Either way, you should now be turning right onto the road that heads south into Brough. Further along, this route is known as Batham Gate as it follows the course of the Roman road from Navio to Buxton.

Cross the river and, after a hundred metres, take the footpath across the field on the right. Up on the hillside, a stile and information board lead you into the field occupied by the Roman fort of Navio. You can see the remains of a wall near the fence and some carved masonry in the centre of the field. If you look closely you should be able to make out earthworks in and around the area of the fort. There were several phases of rebuilding but in the last, during the third and fourth centuries, the north-eastern half, the praetentura comprised six barrack blocks. In the south-west, the retentura, the headquarters, commander's house and granaries were rebuilt in stone.

Although there is now little to see of Navio (or Anavio as it is sometimes known), it was clearly an important Roman fort. There were two distinct periods of occupation, the first between about AD75-120 and the second resuming some forty years later and remaining in use for two hundred years. A civilian community or vicus grew alongside the fort. Such developments are common, providing living accommodation for the soldiers' families (many would have married local Britons) and service industries to support the fort and its occupants. It is unclear exactly what form the Roman occupation would have taken in the Peak District and whether Navio was an active army base or simply more of a settlement but it has been suggested that its main function was to supervise nearby lead-mining activities.

There have been several excavations at Navio since the beginning of the twentieth century. Early work by John Garstang revealed a stepped underground strong-room as well as the fort wall, a tower and internal principia. Later digging by Richmond and Gillam in 1938 and by Manchester University in the 1950s and 60s produced lead ingots. Navio was linked by road to Buxton by Batham Gate and to the fort of Ardotalia, more commonly called Melandra Castle, in Glossop by Doctor's Gate.

A stile at the far side leads on across the fields. The way is a little unclear at some points as stone walls have been removed leaving long open fields. The route lies roughly parallel to the road running along the valley to your right and eventually you should join an obvious trackway cutting diagonally across a field and emerging onto the lane from Bradwell. Here, a bench on the roadside offers a well-earned rest.

Turn right onto the lane and, soon after, turn left at the junction. After a further hundred metres you have a choice of routes. You can either continue along the lane (it is little used and there is minimal traffic) or you can take the footpath across the fields on your right, signposted to Castleton. I would suggest that walkers doing the shorter route should take the road and return along the footpath. The road passes the restored building of Pindale Mine (now part of an outdoor pursuits centre) and leads into the south of Castleton near the castle.

➡️*Walkers following route 19a rejoin here*

Castleton is a planned town, set out in Medieval times in the shadow of Peveril Castle. It centres around a market place and the long strips of early field systems are still evident around the perimeter. Peveril Castle is managed by English Heritage and you can look round it for a small fee. Originally built in timber, with two baileys, its position on the natural clifftop meant it did not need a motte. It was first built by William Peveril, rebuilt in stone in the mid-late twelfth century. Peveril Castle was an administrative centre for the Peak Forest and associated lead mining. Castleton is also famous for its show caves and for the mining of Blue John, a type of fluorspar found in the hillside to the west of the town. The name is a corruption of the French 'bleu-jeune' describing the characteristic colour of the stone.

➥ *Walkers following the shorter route 19b should return to those directions now*

After you have finished looking round Castleton, turn left onto the main road. A short distance after the chapel and before the last of the buildings, take the path on the right. This crosses fields, for a time following the course of Odin Sitch, and emerges at the Odin Mine ore crushing circle. Alternatively, you can simply follow the road past Treak Cliff Cavern to the parking area.

Finding out more:

Garlick T 1975 *Roman Derbyshire* (Dalesman Publishing)

Garstang J 1904 *DAJ*

Jones G D B & F H Thompson 1965 'Excavations at Mam Tor and Brough-on-Noe' *DAJ*

Makepeace G A 1994 'Back Tor: A Bronze Age site in Edale, Derbyshire' *DAJ*

Preston, F 1954 'The hill-forts of the Peak' *DANHSJ* Vol 74

Walk 19a: Mam Tor and Castleton

Distance: 5 miles (8km).

Starting Point: Odin Mine SK135834. Park your car on the road near to Odin's Mine. This is reached by going west out of Castleton and continuing along the road past Treak Cliff Cavern rather than forking left into Winnat's pass.

Refreshments: There are pubs and cafes in Castleton.

Preamble

This walk takes you to see the Bronze Age and Iron Age remains on Mam Tor followed by a relaxed stroll downhill into Castleton. Once there, you can look round Peveril Castle or join a guided tour down one of the mines open to the public as show caves.

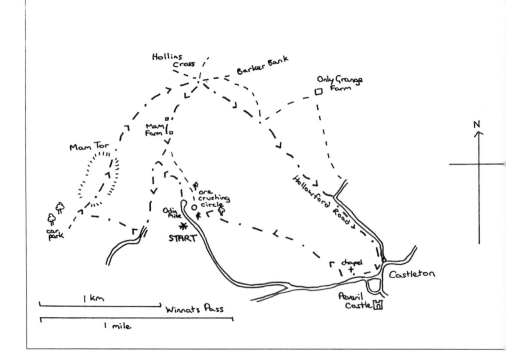

The Walk

➡️***Start the walk at the beginning of the directions for Walk 19.***

From Hollins Cross, paths lead in six directions. You should turn right from the main path from where the first route leads directly back to Odin mine, either branching across fields at Mam Farm or continuing down the farm track to the landslipped road. To walk to Castleton, take the path south-east from Hollins Cross. From here, all routes lead into the town. If you continue straight ahead you will come to a farm track that becomes Hollowford Road, approaching Castleton from the north.

➡️***Rejoin Walk 19 where indicated.***

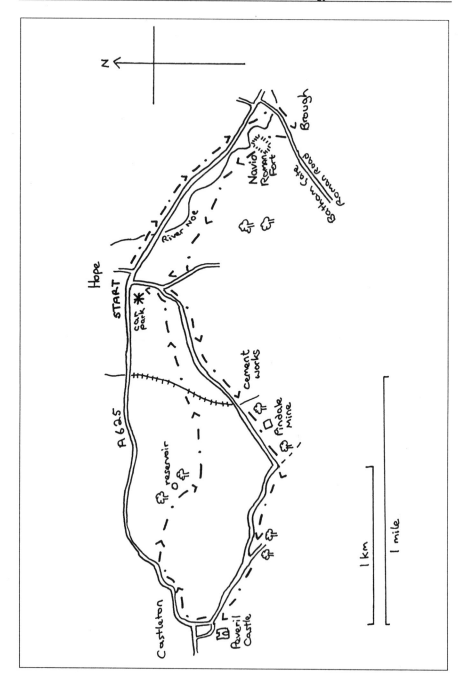

Walk 19b: Castleton and Navio

Distance: 5 miles (8km).

Starting Point: Hope, SK172835. Park in the village of Hope, there is a car park to the south of the main road.

Refreshments: There are pubs and cafes in Castleton and Hope.

Preamble

This walk explores the site of the Roman fort of Navio. The shorter route has the benefit of allowing the walker more time in Castleton to visit Peveril Castle or one of the mines open to the public as show caves.

The Walk

Join the main road and walk due east.

➡️*Follow the directions in Walk 19 where indicated.*

Leave Castleton by the main road walking back towards Hope. Just before the end of the town, take the footpath on the right, across the fields. Soon after the railway you come to a lane. Turn left here and you are back in the centre of Hope with the church on your right and the car park on your left.

Walk 20: Castle Naze and The Bull Ring Henge

Distance: 8 miles (13km).

Starting Point: Chapel en le Frith, SK052804. The walk starts on the west side of the town near the high school.

Refreshments: There are refreshments available at Chapel en le Frith and, to a lesser extent in Dove Holes.

Preamble

This walk visits two of the lesser known yet most impressive archaeological features of the Peak District. At Dove Holes, the Bull Ring henge is of similar dimensions to the famous Arbor Low yet, because it has no stones or perhaps because it is not located in open countryside, it lies almost forgotten beside the busy A6. High above Chapel en le Frith, Castle Naze hillfort is perfect in its simplicity, with huge straight banks and ditches defending the only approach to a clifftop fortress. Pay a visit to the church in Chapel where there is a Danish cross.

The Walk

Start at the west side of Chapel en le Frith in a road called Long Lane, running south from the main street. About a hundred metres down this road, on the right, is a high school and immediately before the school, running alongside it, is a footpath. Follow this footpath, when you reach the housing estate the path bends to the left then the right, leading behind the houses. At one point the path actually cuts through a garden and resumes its route on the opposite side of a landscaped lawn. Eventually you leave the houses behind, turning left to cross a stile into a field then immediately right to follow the line of the hedge. There is part of a golf course in the field on the right and further ahead, following the way across stiles, the route crosses the golf course on two occasions with a grassy field in between.

Having left the golf course behind via the short board walk, the way now turns half left and crosses the fields diagonally until emerging onto a road. Turn left at the road and walk the short distance to where the railway bridge crosses. Immediately after the bridge, turn left and follow the path alongside the embankment. After a quarter of a mile, cross the stile on your right (if you continue the path soon ends at a gate). The next section is not obvious or clearly marked but public footpaths are marked on the ordnance survey map. Recent fencing prevents you from taking the exact course of the path, which should cross the field diagonally. Instead, I suggest you turn left after the stile and follow the course of the railway until you come to a gate on your left, turn right (facing south) and cross the field to the gate opposite. Go through (or over) this gate and a faint track leads up the hillside in an easterly direction. Ignore the padlocked gate at the top of the slope and continue round the hillside to the left of the wall. After you have passed the buildings on your right you come to a break in the wall, go through this and cross the grass to a gate directly ahead which opens onto a roadway. Turn right onto the road (actually more of a drive) and follow it as it bends round to the left between various properties. A stile brings you out onto a narrow lane at the foot of Castle Naze.

On the opposite side of the road is the start of the official path up the steep hillside opposite, the right-hand point of which is Castle Naze Iron Age hillfort. Climb up the path and turn left along the fence. A short distance along a stile gives access to the ditches and banks and the fort enclosure. It is not difficult to see why this location was chosen for fortification, the steep rock faces on two sides of the triangle meant that only one straight line of defence was necessary.

Two and a quarter acres (0.9 hectares) are enclosed by the fortifications and the area had a water supply in the form of a spring; it is not clear, however, whether it was a permanent settlement. It is thought that the fort was built in several phases. In the first phase, probably around 500BC, the west bank – the inner one – was the only defence from the east and the entrance was via a hollow-way

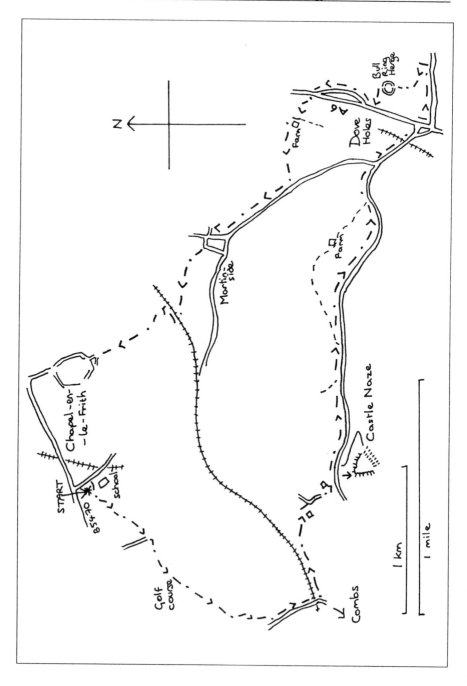

which climbs the hill transversely, emerging near to the stile. In a later phase, the outer bank and ditch were dug. The reason for thinking this is that these outer ramparts are higher than the inner ones, a feature that would be counter-productive defensively. Normally, in the case of multiple banks and ditches, the innermost defences are the highest, enabling the occupants to see potential attackers in advance and to deal with them suitably. It is therefore thought that the outer bank and ditch were intended to replace the earlier ones rather than to supplement them. The entrance from the south-east clearly cuts through the inner bank and ditch making it later than this structure.

Another archaeological theory is that both the transverse path up the hill and the cutting through the bank and ditch are formed by a packhorse route; alternatively, local tradition suggests that the gap in the ramparts is a Roman road. It cannot be the road between Buxton and Glossop as this has been plotted a mile or so to the east. However, surface finds of Roman pottery and a coin were found within the fort.

Return to the lane and turn right. This is a particularly quiet and scenic stretch of road (I saw only one bicycle when I did the walk) and I recommend following this route into Dove Holes. However, if you wish, you can take the second footpath on the left, walking around Cow Low and through Cowlow farm to rejoin the road just before the first houses.

On reaching Dove Holes, turn right and follow the road over the railway bridge. Continue down to the crossroads, taking care while crossing the busy A6. As you walk down the road opposite you can see the remains of limestone extraction on the right. After a third of a mile, take the footpath on the left immediately after the last house. Keep to the hedge on the left and cross the stile into a rather barren area of lime workings. You will join a footpath from the main road, turn right at this point and continue walking due north until you reach the large circular earthwork immediately before the football pitch. This is the Bull Ring Henge.

Squeezed between a football pitch and quarrying debris, beside a busy main road, the Bull Ring seems rather sad and forgotten. However, it is clear that it was once a very spectacular monument. The

Remains of mining and quarrying at Dove Holes

diameter of the circle is similar to that of Arbor Low although the surrounding bank is not as high, but this is probably due to erosion of the bank and silting up of the ditch. It is likely that a circle of stones once stood within the henge but these have been removed. The Bull Ring was excavated by Alcock in 1949 revealing Neolithic pottery, so the monument may be older than Arbor Low (which is thought to be Early Bronze Age). A man-made mound or cairn lies immediately to the south-west of the henge although it is a little difficult to identify because of all the quarrying. We can only guess for what purpose henges were built. The fact that many have burials either within the structure or nearby suggests that they had ceremonial significance. They may also have been used for more mundane social gatherings.

A geophysical survey was conducted at the Bull Ring in 2000. Two types of investigation were applied. Resistivity survey passes a small electric current between points in the ground and measures electrical resistance. On a computer printout this shows walls, stones and voids at one end of the spectrum and waterlogged soil at the other. Magnetometry detects variations in the magnetic property of the soil, it can show buried stones and areas of burning. It was hoped to find evidence of a stone circle, either the stones themselves or pits where they would have been set. However, there has been so much disturbance and damage to the site over the years that results were inconclusive.

From the sports pavilion, turn left and rejoin the A6. Turn right and follow the service road north. Just a few metres after this ends, take the footpath signposted to the left. Follow the farm track across the fields and bending round to the right. The way on here is a little unclear but basically you need to turn left (due west) between the farm buildings and head straight across the field to a stile. Continue straight ahead and you will come to a road. Turn right and follow the road north-west, bearing right at the fork. Take the next turning on the left at Paradise Farm, crossing the stile to bear right diagonally across the field. Half way across the next field, join the track on your right, turning left towards the buildings ahead. Ignore the track branching to the left and instead continue directly ahead – for the second time on this walk the path leads through a garden. A hollowed track (probably a major route several centuries ago) continues on the far side and leads to the railway. Turn right immediately after the railway bridge and follow the trackway into the next field. The footpath turns left, following the left-hand field boundary on the north side of the stream for a short distance, then crosses to the right-hand side, following this hedge round, bending round to the right, to emerge onto a farm drive. Follow this track to the left until you reach the first houses. From here, the main road through Chapel is due north.

Finding out more:

Barnatt J 1988 'Excavations at the Bull Ring henge, Dove Holes, Derbyshire 1984-5' *DAJ*

Preston, F 1954 'The hill-forts of the Peak' *DANHSJ* Vol 74

Ramm, H 1957 'A Survey of the Combs Moss hill-fort' *DANHSJ*

Wroe, P & P Mellor 1971 'A Roman road between Buxton and Melandra Castle, Glossop' *DAJ*

www.eng-h.gov.uk/reports/bullring/ 'the Bull Ring, Dove Holes, Derbyshire' Report on geophysical survey, September 2000

Walk 21: Torside Castle and Doctor's Gate

Distance: 14 miles (22km).

Starting Point: Glossop, SK043948. Park in Glossop. I recommend leaving your car in Old Glossop near to Manor Park, as this is where the walk finishes.

Refreshments: There are refreshments available in Glossop but take plenty of food and drink with you.

Alternative Routes: There is no short cut to the round trip over the moors. However, with a street plan of Glossop and/or the relevant O.S. map you could visit Mouselow Castle, Ardotalia (Melandra Castle) and stroll up Doctor's Gate.

Preamble

This is a full day walk for the serious outdoor enthusiast and should not be undertaken lightly. It includes part of the remote moorland of the Dark Peak where there are often no visible paths, it is therefore essential to take a map (Ordnance Survey Outdoor Leisure 1, The Peak District, Dark Peak area), a compass and a torch. Allow plenty of time, the walk is likely to take around eight hours but could be more or less depending on your fitness, weather conditions and how often you get lost! Take plenty of food and a flask of hot drink, water-proofs and an extra layer of clothes. Go with a companion and tell someone at home where you are going and when you expect to be back.

The walk visits the definite archaeological sites of Mouselow Castle and Doctor's Gate and the rather less certain one of Torside Castle. The Roman fort of Ardotalia is situated at Gamesley just south of the A57 Manchester Road about two and a half miles west of Glossop centre. I have not included it in the route as it would add an-other five miles to an already long walk. I would suggest instead that those interested should drive there after completing the walk if daylight permits.

The Walk

From Old Glossop, make your way west, crossing the B6105 to Crowden then turning right onto North Road, towards Padfield, and left towards the hospital. Immediately after a left-hand bend, take the unmarked footpath on the right, opposite the hospital gate. Having passed the house on your left, cross the stile on your right and head due east up the hill, emerging, at some buildings, onto a track. Follow the track north, forking to the right at the mast.

The mound beside the mast is known as Mouselow Castle and it is believed to be a damaged motte. Dating to Norman times, a motte, fortified by a bank, would have accommodated a keep in the form of a wooden tower. Such a structure, combined with a larger enclosure on adjacent lower ground – a bailey – would form the basis of an early castle.

Features like that at Mouselow, where there are traces of a motte but no accompanying bailey are harder to interpret. There are several possibilities; that the castle was left unfinished, that a bailey was built but is now too damaged to be traced or that the site is an earlier Norman feature known as a ringwork.

Follow the track round until it joins North Road, turning left into Cemetery Road. There are several ways to get to the Longdendale Trail. You can continue straight ahead down Park Road to the station, alternatively, turn immediately right into Redgate, follow the road as it turns sharp left into Padfield then take the lane on the right. After a few hundred metres, turn right at the T-junction then take the pathway almost immediately on the left. After about a quarter of a mile, take the first path on the left to join the Longdendale Trail. You can now make the most of two and a half miles of easy walking along the course of the disused railway with scenic views of the reservoirs to your left.

At the third dam, the trail crosses the road and you should turn right onto the Pennine Way which is clearly signposted. The first part of the path is paved and steps aid the steep climb up onto

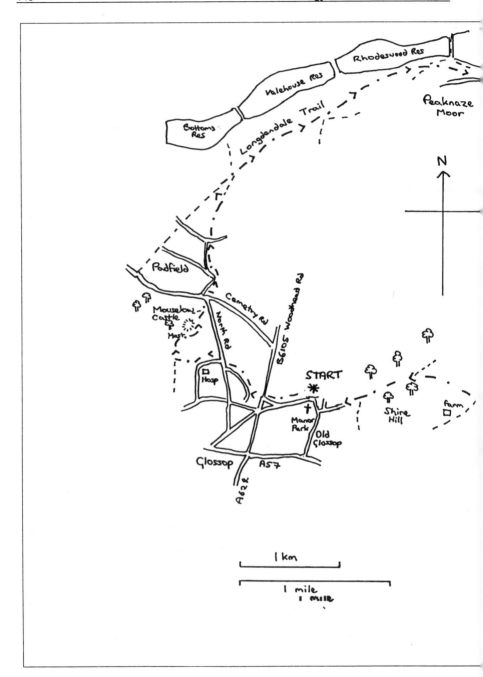

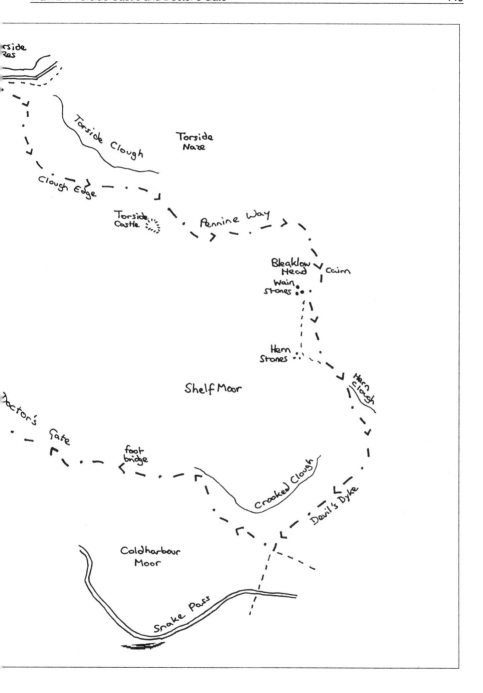

Clough Edge with views of Torside Clough down to your left. The path curves to the left, following the edge and crossing small streams here and there. As you reach the top of the clough, just as the path bends to the right, this is the time for a diversion to visit Torside Castle.

Torside Castle is something of a mystery. It is a low hill that rises above otherwise flat and featureless moorland. The natural watercourse to the west of the hill has carved a ditch resembling the defences of Iron Age enclosures and an area of three-quarters of an acre is enclosed by a single bank. There have been suggestions that it is an Iron Age hillfort and others that it is a ringwork dating to Norman times, similar to that in Hathersage (see walk 18) and possibly Mouselow. Alternatively, it could be a natural feature.

You may wonder why anyone would want to build a monument in such a bleak place but it is important to remember that the terrain did not always look like this. It is thought that the high moorlands of the Dark Peak were once wooded but that the land was deforested and peat began to form during the Mesolithic. Until this time, approximately 8000 years ago, Britain was joined to Europe by a land bridge; this North European Plain disappeared as the sea level rose with the melting of the ice. People would have lived in small groups, feeding themselves by hunting, gathering and fishing; they were probably semi-nomadic, moving to different places at different times of the year. In areas of high ground where the peat has eroded, flint tools have been found. These would typically be leaf shaped arrowheads and tiny blades known as microliths, thought to have been mounted in wood or antler to make implements for threshing and cutting vegetation. Originally, archaeologists thought that Mesolithic people were simple hunters who lived by following herds of deer. Now, with more evidence from well-preserved sites, it is clear that they were skilled craftsmen who knew how to manage their environment.

Rejoin the Pennine Way. After this, the navigation becomes rather more challenging. The route turns sharply to the east for almost a mile, then turns right heading south. The Wain Stones on Bleaklow Head are an obvious landmark to head for if you get lost. South of these, you may find yourself inadvertently passing the

Hern Stones before joining Hern Clough. The path follows the course of this stream until the watercourse turns to the east, here the way continues south before turning south-west along Devil's Dyke Drain.

The course of the Roman road of Doctor's Gate

Half a mile before Snake Pass (you can see the road just ahead), Doctor's Gate crosses the Pennine Way. Turn right and follow the path as it descends down to the Clough, keeping to the hillside on the left until the footbridge. Doctor's Gate is part of the Roman road linking the forts of Navio in Brough and Ardotalia (the original Roman name for Melandra Castle) in Glossop. Unlike Navio, which was occupied for three centuries, Ardotalia has a much shorter history. It was first established in AD80, built of turf and timber – the walls would have been formed from cut turf and all the buildings within made of wood. It was later rebuilt with stone walls and towers and extra defensive ditches dug, the barrack blocks, accommodating five hundred infantry were made of timber. The fort was abandoned in AD140 but it remains the best preserved in the area.

Further to the east the present day road still follows part of this route. The way becomes easier now and soon returns to cultivated land. Take the right fork and follow the track round Shire Hill, arriving back into Old Glossop near to Manor Park.

You will hopefully have time to visit the Roman fort of Ardotalia before you leave Glossop. It is out the other side of town so you may prefer to drive. If you leave the centre on the A57 towards Manchester, Melandra is signposted from the Gamesley housing estate, which is about two miles out on the left-hand side of the road. The plan of the fort was similar to Navio, with the barrack blocks of the praetentura taking up the north-east half and the headquarters in the retentura to the south-west. The bath house was sited outside the main area of the fort on the north-east side. A vicus, an adjacent civilian settlement was sited to the south-east (probably, to a large extent, in the area of the housing estate). Cremation burials were found further out beyond the vicus and outside the ditch and rampart – burials were not allowed within forts according to Roman rule.

Finding out more:

Brassington M 1981 'Roman roads of Derbyshire' *DAJ*

Petch J 1960 'Melandra Castle excavations' *DAJ*

Webster P 1971 'Melandra Castle Roman fort: Excavations in the civil settlement 1966-69' *DAJ*

Useful Addresses and Phone Numbers

Buxton Museum: 01298 24658

Derbyshire Busline: 01298 23098

Derbyshire Caving Association: c/o 3, Greenway, Hulland Ward, Ashbourne, Derbyshire DE6 3FE

Edale Weather Centre Services: 01433 670207

Peak District Mining Museum: South Parade, Matlock Bath, Derbyshire

Peak District National Park Authority: Aldern House, Baslow Road, Bakewell, Derbyshire DE45 1AE

Sheffield City Museum: Weston Park, Sheffield. Tel. 0114 2768588

South Yorkshire Traveline: 01709 515151

Trent Buses: 01332 292200

Glossary

articulated (burial)   one in which bones are still linked or in appropriate position in skeleton indicating that the body was buried intact.

bailey   enclosed area surrounding or adjacent to a castle, see motte and bailey.

barrow   man-made mound (usually) containing burial(s) **long barrow, bank barrow** – usually Neolithic; **round barrow** – usually Bronze Age.

beaker   finely crafted and decorated pot, the design originating in Europe, found in Britain during the early Bronze Age. Also refers to the culture of bronze-working etc that is associated with these ceramics.

bole   an ore smelting hearth, usually on top of a hill.

Bronze Age   the period in prehistory approximately 2000-700BC (in Britain) roughly corresponding with the introduction of bronze working.

cairn   mound formed of rocks. From the Neolithic onwards, sometimes to clear the land, often covering a burial. In non-archaeological sense cairns are also built by walkers as way-markers.

cairnfield   an area with numerous cairns.

cap stone   large slab forming the roof of a chambered tomb or passage grave.

chambered tomb   usually dating to the Neolithic, structure made of stone slabs, containing the bones of the dead. Sometimes had several compartments or chambers into which different combinations of bones were arranged. The whole was originally covered by a mound or cairn.

cremation   burial of burnt bone.

cup and ring   Neolithic and Early Bronze Age decorations of circular depressions and spirals pecked into stone.

Derbyshire ware   a style of pottery produced in the southern part of the Peak District in Roman times.

disarticulated (burial)	collection of bones no longer attached – often indicates that the body was excarnated or defleshed prior to burial.
faience	an early type of glass, often coloured blue, found in Bronze Age burials in the form of cylindrical or star-shaped beads.
fibula	Roman pinned brooch.
field system	remnants of ancient ploughing indicated by banks of earth (lynchets) or walled divisions of fields and pens.
food vessel	decorated Early Bronze Age pot often found with burials.
henge	circular earthwork of bank(s) and ditch(es), dating to the late Neolithic and Early Bronze Age (approximately 2000BC).
hillfort	enclosure on hill top, defended by ramparts. Defences usually date to the Iron Age though the site may have been occupied before this.
Holocene	the current interglacial period.
hornwork	the curving facade often found forming a forecourt to chambered tombs. The whole resembles an insect with horns/antennae.
inhumation	burial typically either extended (lying flat) or in a crouched position (often dating to the late Neolithic or Early Bronze Age).
Iron Age	the last period of British prehistory approximately 700BC – AD50. Historically associated with production of iron goods.
low	a conical shaped hill or a barrow – most often a barrow on top of a hill.
lynchet	bank of earth formed by ancient systems of ploughing.
Mesolithic	the period in prehistory approximately 8000-4000BC associated with hunter-gatherer-fishers.
microliths	very small flint implements dating to the Mesolithic and thought to form composite tools.
motte and bailey	early form of castle comprising a man-made defensible hill (motte) and enclosure (bailey).

Neolithic
literally the new stone age, the period in Britain approximately 4000-2000BC associated with the introduction of farming.

orthostat
standing stone, often part of larger monument.

Palaeolithic
literally the old stone age. Anything before the retreat of the ice approximayely 10000 years ago.

passage grave
a type of chambered tomb, characterised architecturally by construction of entrance passage leading to burial chamber(s).

Pleistocene
the geological time of ice ages preceding the current interglacial (Holocene).

pygmy cup
small ceramic vessel found in Later Neolithic/Early Bronze Age burials. The open lattice design would make it unsuitable for liquids so it may have been used for solids such as aromatic herbs.

quernstone
millstone.

rake
a vein of ore, often vertical.

ringcairn
a circular bank of stones/rubble without standing stones.

Romano-British
native British people (or associated artefacts) living under Roman occupation. Roman usually refers to villas or forts associated with the Roman army or to imported goods.

saddle quern
early type of millstone in the shape of a saddle used in prehistoric periods.

scrapers
small flint implements often dating to the Neolithic and Bronze Age and used for e.g. skinning animals.

sough
a mine adit or tunnel dug for drainage.

vicus
civilian settlement adjacent to a Roman fort.

wristguard
rectangular object, usually stone, strapped against the wrist for protection when drawing a bow. Found in Bronze Age burials.

Index

A

Aldwark 50
Alport 61
Alstonefield 17
Anglo-Saxon 5, 89, 124, 133
  burials 35
  crosses 35, 108
  field systems 92
Arbor Low 3, 54 - 59, 111, 140, 144
Ardotalia 134, 146, 151 - 152

B

Back Tor 132
barrows 2, 5, 8, 12 - 13, 17, 20 - 22, 29 - 31, 33, 44, 46 - 47, 75, 100, 131
Baslow Edge 108
Beakers 3, 13, 29, 32, 39, 51, 53
Beeley Moor 97, 99, 101
Birchen Edge 103
Birchover 61, 70
Blue John 134
Bole Hill 118, 123
Bolehill Quarry 122
Bradbourne 34 - 37
Brassington 38
Bronze Age 3
  burials 83, 155, 157
  pottery 104
Bull Ring Henge 140 - 145

C

Camp Green 120, 125 - 126
Carl Wark 120 - 125
Castle Naze 82, 140 - 145
Castle Ring 61, 67 - 68, 73
castles 23, 28, 74 - 75, 127, 134
chambered tombs 84 - 85, 93
Chapel en le Frith 140
Chee Tor 84 - 91, 95
Chelmorton 93
Cheshire Wood Cave 20
Conksbury 74 - 78
copper mines 9
Crane's Fort 74 - 78
Cronkston 27
Cross Low 29
Crowdecote 28
Curbar Edge 110

D

Danish crosses 17, 140

Dark Ages 5
Deepdale 84 - 91
Derbyshire Ware 5
Doctor's Gate 134, 146 - 151
Doll Tor 61, 70 - 72

E

Eaglestone Flat 108, 113
Ecton Hill 9 - 15
Elder Bush Cave 13, 15
excarnation 35
Eyam 114
Eyam Moor 114 - 119

F

faience beads 71
Falcon Low Cave 20
field systems 44, 46, 92, 95, 108, 110 - 111, 123, 134
Fin Cop 79, 81 - 83
Five Wells 21, 41, 84 - 93
Fox Hole Cave 23 - 25, 27
Froggatt 119

G

Gardom's Edge 103 - 107
Gib Hill 58
Glossop 146
granges 6, 27, 43, 45, 47, 49, 56, 75, 89
Green Low
  Aldwark 41, 43, 50
  Eaton & Alsop 29, 32

H

Harborough Rocks 34, 38 - 42
Harland Edge 99
Harthill Moor 61 - 69, 73
Hathersage 120 - 125
henges 3, 58, 102, 144
hillforts 4, 61, 67, 81, 131
Hob Hurst's House 97
Hulme End 9

I

Iron Age 4

K

Kniveton 34

L

Lathkill Dale 54, 75
Lathkill Head Cave 56

lead mines 15
Liff's Low 29, 32
Long Low 17, 19, 21
Longnor 23
Lose Hill 132

M

Mam Tor 127 - 137
Mandale Mine 74, 77
Manifold Valley 9 - 16
medieval manors 108
medieval villages 74, 78
Mesolithic 2
microliths 2
Middleton Castle 75
Milldale 17
Miller's Dale 95
Minning Low 34 - 35, 41, 43 - 51, 85, 88
Monsal Head 79
Monyash 54
motte and bailey 5, 28
Mouselow Castle 147

N

Navio 127 - 136, 139, 151
Needham 27
Neolithic 2
    artefacts 24
    burials 3, 13 - 14, 20 - 21, 58
    chambered tombs 43, 50, 85
    decoration 107, 118
    pottery 23, 144
Net Low/Nettly Knowe 32
Nine Ladies stone circle 61, 65
Nine Stone Close 61, 68, 73
Norman 5

O

Odin Mine 127
One Ash Grange 56, 60
One Ash village 56
orthostats 65
Ossum's Cave 14

P

Padley Chapel 108, 111, 120 - 123
Padley Gorge 123
Park Gate 101
Peveril Castle 5, 134
Pilsbury 27
Pilsbury Castle 23 - 28
Pindale Mine 134

Q

querns 90, 122

R

Rain's Cave 39
Rainster Rocks 34, 38 - 42
reindeer, remains of 14
Reynard's Cave 17, 19, 21
ringcairns 65, 102, 114, 119
Ringham Low 54 - 59
ringworks 5
rock art 106 - 107, 114
Roman 4
    artefacts 24, 89
    forts 127, 133, 139, 146
    lead mining 39, 91, 127
    pottery 90, 143
    roads 48, 133, 143, 151 - 152
Romano-British settlements 4, 5, 38 - 39,
    43 - 44, 46, 83 - 84, 95
Roystone Grange 43 - 49

S

Slipper Low 53
Stanton Moor 61 - 72
Stoke Flat 108, 110
stone circles 3, 8, 52, 58, 61, 64 - 65,
    70 - 71, 73, 108, 110, 114, 116
Stoney Low 43, 50, 52
Swainsley copper mine 10
Swine Sty 110

T

Thirst Hole Cave 89
Thor's Cave 13 - 14
Thor's Fissure Cave 13
Throwley Hall 20
Torside Castle 146 - 151

U

Upper Padley 120 - 125
Upper Palaeolithic 1

V

vici 133, 152

W

Wet Withens 114, 116 - 117
Wetton 16
Wetton Mill 14
White Peak 2
Wigber Low 34 - 35, 37

Y

Youlgreave 73 - 74

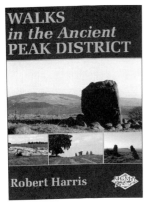

WALKS IN THE ANCIENT PEAK DISTRICT
Robert Harris

The third in this successful series, Walks in the Ancient Peak District is a collection of walks visiting the prehistoric monuments and sites of the Peak District, including the White Peak, Dark Peak, Western and Eastern Moors. Explore rock shelters and caves of the old stone age, stone circles and burial chambers of the Neolithic and Bronze Ages and the great hill forts of the Iron Age, whilst appreciating the beautiful scenery and wildlife of the Peak District. £8.95

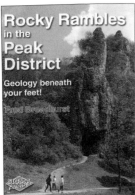

ROCKY RAMBLES IN THE PEAK DISTRICT: Geology Beneath Your Feet
Fred Broadhurst

"The Peak District has a dramatic story to tell and Fred Broadhurst is just the guide we need." – Aubrey Manning, presenter of BBC TV 'Earth Story'.
Imagine the glaciers, volcanoes and landslips that shaped the Peak District; see for yourself the fossils of ancient plants and animals that formed beneath its vast seas; find the remains of mineral mines. Details and descriptions of where to find these – and much more – are included in these 18 walks with maps, information on parking and refreshments. £7.95

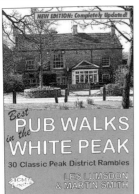

BEST PUB WALKS IN THE WHITE PEAK
and
BEST PUB WALKS IN THE DARK PEAK
Les Lumsdon & Martin Smith

These two volumes – White Peak and Dark Peak – are designed to provide the most comprehensive coverage. Without doubt, the longest established and most authoritative guidebooks of their kind. Both books completely updated.
£7.95 each.

All of our books are available from your local bookshop. In case of difficulty, or to obtain our complete catalogue, contact: **Sigma Leisure, 5 Alton Road, Wilmslow, Cheshire SK9 5DY**

Tel/Fax: 01625-531035.   E-mail: info@sigmapress.co.uk   Web site: www.sigmapress.co.uk